Boris Röhrl

Marxist Philosophy and Art History

EINFÜHRUNGEN
– Philosophie –

INTRODUCTION
– Philosophy –

Band/volume 24

LIT

Boris Röhrl

Marxist Philosophy and Art History

Introduction, Development, Terminology

LIT

This book is printed on acid-free paper.

Bibliographic information published by the Deutsche Nationalbibliothek
The Deutsche Nationalbibliothek lists this publication in the Deutsche Nationalbibliografie; detailed bibliographic data are available on the Internet at http://dnb.d-nb.de.

ISBN 978-3-643-91003-5

A catalogue record for this book is available from the British Library

Klosbachstr. 107
CH-8032 Zürich
Tel. +41 (0) 44-251 75 05
E-Mail: zuerich@lit-verlag.ch http://www.lit-verlag.ch
Distribution:
In the UK: Global Book Marketing, e-mail: mo@centralbooks.com
In North America: International Specialized Book Services, e-mail: orders@isbs.com
In Germany: LIT Verlag Fresnostr. 2, D-48159 Münster
Tel. +49 (0) 2 51-620 32 22, Fax +49 (0) 2 51-922 60 99, e-mail: vertrieb@lit-verlag.de

e-books are available at www.litwebshop.de

CONTENTS

Sebald Beham, *In the Peasants' War (Im Bauernkrieg 1525)*,
copperplate engraving, 5,2 x 7,6 cm, 1544,
Museen der Stadt Nürnberg, Graphische Sammlung

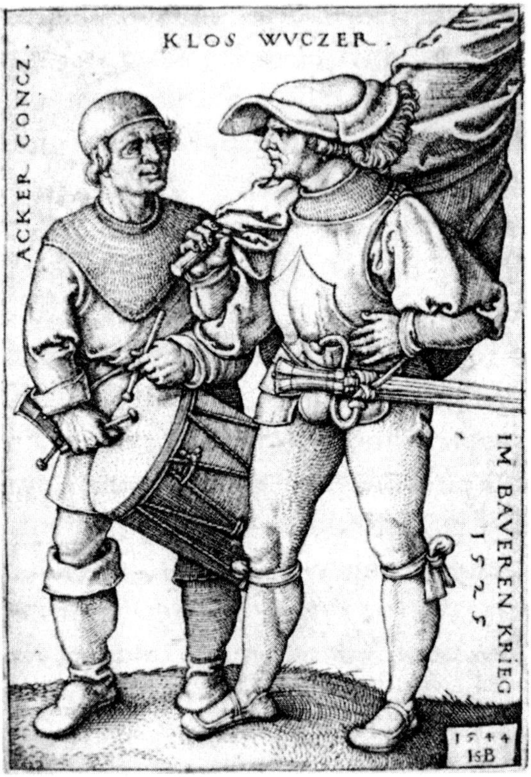

PREFACE

This introduction to Marxist philosophy and art history is conceived as a small reference book. The French original edition of 2016 did not contain an introductory chapter on Marxist philosophy, for it contains a glossary of Marxist terminology with the referring passages at the end. This aside, the French and English editions are identical.

The conception of the manual is as follows: After a very short introduction to Marxist philosophy there are three chapters which expound the application of this philosophy to the discipline of history of art. Thus, the second chapter contains art historical literature with a Marxist imprint and the third, the context of scientific Marxism in relation to other directions of thought that display a partly similar conception and are therefore sometimes confused with it. The manual finishes in the fourth chapter with an elucidation of the different methods of Marxist analysis.

The following text is the result of a controversial discussion that took place over a long period of time and during which the manuscript was criticized in nearly all of its aspects. This text was even criticized as being non-Marxist in its entire structure, and, indeed this is the case, since a scientific text is not a political pamphlet; it should present things in a neutral way so that readers with different outlooks are able to obtain information.

A second misunderstanding arose concerning the subject of this manual. It deals with classical Marxism and its relationship to art history; it does not have the aim of confronting the reader with the wide field of critical theory and similar related directions of thought, nor does it address the equally expansive field of art theory. During the discussion I became aware of the multiplicity of contemporary Marxist movements, which differ among themselves even between countries. The majority of these directions do not seem to be related to Marxist thought inside the workers' movement. Today, the different movements inspired by Marxism seem to have no common denominator. Nevertheless, I have attempted to give a shortlist of international literature, which is restricted to only a few names. This list belongs to a more or less accepted canon, and it provides an idea of the development of Marxism in the field of art history up to the end of the twentieth century.

Boris Röhrl — Wiesbaden, March 2018

1. INTRODUCTION TO MARXIST PHILOSOPHY

•

Marx united different philosophical, sociological and economic theories of the eighteenth and nineteenth centuries in a new philosophy, which explains the behavior of human beings in society. Marxism is a revolutionary theory. It does not reflect upon historical evolution in an abstract, idealistic way, but it is thought to encourage the human being to actively intervene in the present. One can identify the analytical and agitatorial elements of this philosophy, but it is not possible to separate them from each other. Marxism presents a new model of explaining the world, which adopted the following in a changed manner, sometimes as anti-theses: German idealism (Friedrich Hegel), French literature on social order (Henri de Saint-Simon, Auguste Comte), the writings of French physiocrats of the eighteenth century and classical economics (David Ricardo, Adam Smith, John Stuart Mill).

The nucleus of Marxism is the concept of political economy, which constitutes the basics of all other components of this philosophy. Therefore, the three volumes of the *Capital* occupy a central position in understanding Marx's work. Today, some elements of his way of reasoning seem to be outdated, but the core of Marx's statements is more relevant than ever, since in the twenty-first century, capitalism is not counter-balanced by an opposing force and therefore the prognoses of Marx begin to come into effect with full force.

We would therefore recommend prioritizing the writings by Marx himself and not the many interpretations from the twentieth century. Marx's original manuscripts are written in nineteenth-century German, and the meaning of central terms is very different from current German semantics, which complicates the full comprehension of these texts by a non-academic German audience. The situation is much better regarding native speakers of English, since there are modern translations of an extremely high quality, such as *Marx Engels Collected Works*. Regarding Germany, it would be necessary to translate Marx's writings into modern German, but every transference into contemporary German would be an interpretation and therefore this idea seems somewhat inadequate.

Which are the most important books written by Marx? A manuscript that provides readers with a direct insight into the different considerations of Marx and Engels regarding the creation of a philosophy of critical thought, which date back to around 1845 and 1846. In the nineteenth century, this manuscript was not published. In the course of the twentieth century it was released under the title *The German Ideology*[1], though it would have been more convenient to publish it under the title "The Bourgeois Ideology", since it describes the anatomy of bourgeois thought and of bourgeois society. A very short, common access is offered by *Manifesto of the Communist Party* (1848).[2] Class theory plays a central role in all of Marx's writings, and in a very pronounced form in *The Eighteenth Brumaire of Louis Bonaparte* (1852)[3] which certainly needs to be interpreted in a figurative sense and is hardly comprehensible without knowledge of the history of the French revolution of 1848/49. The class formations and mechanisms described here remain valid until the present day. Political economy is the key to understanding Marxism. Marxism must be understood with the priority of economics over all other aspects. The state of economics, as well as the state of technological development, influences all areas of the human existence. Access to Marx's economic theories is presented in the three volumes of the *Capital*; studying this work must logically begin with the first volume entitled *Capital. The Process of Production of Capital* (1867).[4] However, it is precisely this main work on political economy which makes access difficult for the general public. It is for this reason that several popular summaries and simplified versions for workers have been published over the last 150 years.

Marxist philosophy is introduced in this very brief summary by presenting four main theories: Marxist political economy, class theory, historical materialism and Marx's ideas on base and superstructure.

1.1. POLITICAL ECONOMY

Political economy constitutes the very core of Marxist philosophy, which sees society essentially guided by economic activities (agriculture, trade and industry) of its epoch: primitive forms of economics correspond to a simple social order, whereas a higher developed economic system automatically

---

[1] *The German Ideology*, in *MECW 5*.

[2] *Manifesto of the Communist Party*, in *MECW 6*, pp. 477–519.

[3] *The Eighteenth Brumaire of Louis Bonaparte*, in *MECW 11*, pp. 99–197.

[4] *Capital. Vol 1*, in *MECW 35*.

produces a more complex social structure. Analysis of society cannot be separated from the primacy of economics. All aspects of economic activity are intertwined with the organization of human society, and it is not possible to analyze them detached from each other. If one wants to explain certain phenomena of society, the state of economic development must be examined first, since changes in the system of economics bring changes to society as a consequence.

The whole life of the individual is determined by material production. Because certain goods are produced, human beings form certain relationships to each other, and certain patterns within society develop. It is not possible to escape these relations of production. Human beings invent certain notions which conceal this process of production and their own state of captivation within this process. It is the material process of production that creates religious, political and cultural ideas. Intellectual production is indissolubly connected with material production. Marx's central statement is:

> The mode of production of material life conditions the general process of social, political and intellectual life. It is not the consciousness of men that determines their existence, but their social existence that determines their consciousness.[5]

The aim of Marxist philosophy is to lay bare the reality of social relations. Since the economy is the motor of society, Marx described the entirety of institutions and procedures which enable people to produce and distribute goods. This is because the *relations of production* (*Produktionsverhältnisse*) occupy a central place in Marxist economic theory (plate 1). They are the objective, decisive factor that forms the basis of all human societies. These relations of production are defined as the conditions under which food, goods, commercial services, etc., are produced. These relations of production are influenced by various factors such as the structure of society, forces of production, principles of law, techniques of communication, and other relationships created by man. Also vice versa, these relations of production exercise a negative or positive influence on the productive forces. Another expression which Marx frequently uses is "mode of production" (*Produktionsweise*), which he employed in a very wide sense, often linked with "relations of production". In Marx's German writings the word "production" (*Produktion*) is used synonymously for "relations of production or "modes of production."

Relations of production

Modes of production

The nucleus of relations of production is *tools of production* (*Produktionsinstrumente*), which are the concrete instruments with which things are produced (agricultural tools, machines, etc.). The unity of these tools is called *means of production* (*Produktionsmittel*), which means arable soil, machinery, energy, etc. Means of production combined with labor power are termed *forces of production*, or *productive forces* (*Produktivkräfte*), which also includes the level of education of workers and similar factors. In

Means of production

[5] Karl Marx and Friedrich Engels, *The German Ideology* (1846/47), in *MECW* 5, 263.

Pl. 1 Central terms of Marxist economic theory

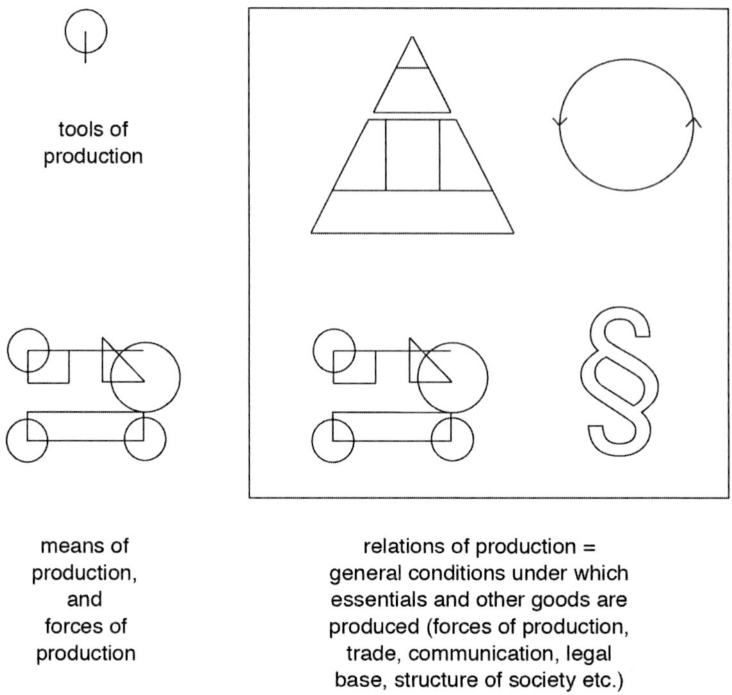

his economic writings in German, Marx's use of the terms "means of production" and "forces of production" is sometimes not easy to distinguish. Sometimes, he speaks of *materielle Produktionskräfte* ("material forces of production") and this cannot include labor power.

Forces of production

Means and forces of production are the decisive factor upon which society is built. They are the material conditions and techniques which help to produce things and social actions. In ancient societies, farming equipment and artisan techniques were at a primitive stage. Since productive forces were at a low stage of development, society displayed a simple structure. As a law, productive forces show the natural tendency to evolve further, since the work of every generation is built on the results of the work of former generations.

A certain social structure can support the development of higher productive forces, while another social order can prevent further evolution. Relations of production have a positive or negative effect on productive forces. Of course, older and newer modes of production can exist in different geographical regions at the same time.

The mode of production influences all spheres of human life. It is a decisive factor from which humans cannot escape. For instance, the hierarchy of human society is not a stable factor, but rather changes according to the development of productive forces. The invention of new technologies causes a further development of relations of production, and therefore leads to changes in the order of society. Since early civilizations, economics have been based on the *division of labor*. Every human being takes on a fixed role in the process of production. A highly developed economy is necessarily based on a very complex structure of human labor. The division of labor explains the division of society into different classes. Since it is possible to analyze and accurately describe the process of production, it is equally possible to describe the structure of society as inherently related to a historical or contemporary stage of economics.

In connection with this thought, a short passage in *German Ideology* is of central significance regarding all disciplines of social sciences. Marx explains that the artist, like every other individual, is firmly tied to the economy. The artist and his work are the result of the structure of production. Therefore, the painter like any other professional is not exceptional, he or she could be replaced by others, because all social activities, and this also includes artistic creation, depend on a certain state of economic development: it is precisely this form of economy which brings about certain aesthetical forms. These artistic forms exist independently of the individual. To put it in another way, the artist is only the performer of a subordinated mode of production. Marx explained this using the example of Raphael, who had been adored as a God-like genius in the nineteenth century:

> Raphael as much as any other artist was determined by the technical advances in art made before him, by the organization of society and the division of labor in his locality, and, finally, by the division of labor in all the countries with which his locality had intercourse. Whether an individual like Raphael succeeds in developing his talent depends wholly on demand, which in turn depends on the division of labor and the conditions of human culture resulting from it.[6]

Another central theory of Marxist economics is as follows: if society, and therefore cultural production, is based on the material process of production, this evokes the question as to what different forms of economics existed in the past and present. To explain this, Marx constructed four models of economics. These models are often simplified into supratemporal schemes that describe a characteristic formation that does not entirely fit with a real formation. These models are "designated as epochs that mark the economic progress,"[7] for they replaced older, inefficient forms of economics.

---

[6] Ibid., 393.

[7] Karl Marx, *A Contribution to the Critique of Political Economy* (Preface) (1859), in *MECW* 29, 263.

Different modes of production

In specific epochs of human history and in different geographical regions, there were different relations of production which can be described. One can distinguish between *Asiatic, ancient, feudal and modern bourgeois (capitalist) modes of production.*[8] In literature, the expression "mode of production" is often simplistically replaced with "society." This kind of abridgement is a little misleading, since the specific structure of society is an output of a certain mode of production. Marx's "slaveholder society" is not the same as his "ancient mode of production," since the first corresponds with historical reality, whereas the latter is an abstract description of a model of economics.

Asiatic mode of production

The expression "*Asiatic mode of production*" is not specifically related to that part of the world but must be interpreted in a figurative sense. Marx also speaks of "*oriental despotism*," but this political catchword does not enlighten what is defined as "Asiatic production." Even though Marx counted it as one of the four main types of economics, he did not exhaustively describe it in his economic writings. Its definition can, however, be derived from his writings on British colonialism, especially his deliberations on the situation in India. Asiatic production includes all sorts of production in which economics is hindered from developing further due to climatic, sociological, religious and other reasons. A second particular characteristic trait is the state monopoly on certain necessities such as arable land or irrigation systems in regions with a desert climate. There are huge cities, but rather than being centers of material production, they are places that represent state or divine power. All these factors lead to social stagnation. In most cases, the society connected to this mode of production reflects a strict hierarchical order that has been frozen at a certain stage of its historical evolution. Therefore, the population shows a certain impassivity or lethargy, and there are few activities that could lead towards a further development of productive forces.[9] During the twentieth century, the concept of Asiatic production posed some problems to Western as well as Soviet Marxists, since it was seen as a negative pendant to the capitalist mode of production characterized in a positive mood as being "dynamic" by Marx. The debates also concerned the parallels of this model to tsarist Russia. Certain Western Marxists have even recognized some similarities to Soviet economics. Nevertheless, the Asiatic mode of production is an epistemologically important instrument for the analysis of societies in the past and present times.

Ancient mode of production

The "*ancient mode of production*" describes a historical state of economics. There are few efforts to develop the productive forces further (for instance the mechanization of agriculture), since there exists a huge surplus of cheap human labor. There is wide circulation of goods and, seen

---

[8] Ibid.

[9] Karl Marx, "The British Rule in India," *New-York Daily Tribune*, June 25, 1853, no. 3804, in *MECW* 12, 125–133.

as a whole, economics produce a certain surplus. However, this surplus is invested in unproductive things like buildings for religious and state representation or luxury goods. Society is shaped as follows: there is a dominant class which consists of few families, a small class of merchants and artisans in bigger cities and the immense majority of the population without any rights or property. The political power lies in the hands of a few kinship groups. This political system is called "oligarchy." The ancient mode of production corresponds to the level of civilization which is hardly developed.

Feudal mode of production

Described by Marx in many different variants, the "*feudal mode of production*" represents a historical stage of economics which he believes explains the emergence of capitalism.[10] In line with this, he often compared positive and negative aspects of the feudal and capitalist production with each other. According to Marx, European societies of the Middle Ages represented a more advanced level of civilization and economic development compared with antiquity. The human being assumed a much more important role than in the antique world, since there is a certain lack of human labor. Even the serf possessed arable land, albeit often in a restricted manner. Feudal production is connected with agrarian societies with an extremely low circulation of goods. The peasants gave a part of the produced necessities to the feudal landowners, who, in return for this, protected them against enemy threats. The feudal society is organized according to a strictly hierarchical structure. Over the course of centuries, production and trade in the few cities evolved, since there was a demand for goods produced by artisans and furthermore of merchandise from the Orient. Then—Marx did not specify the exact point of time, but today, the twelfth century is regarded as the period of change—a turning point becomes visible: since the population in Europe had grown and there was a greater need for goods, the first attempts to create the capitalist system emerged in the larger mercantile centers. Artisan production and trade assumed increasingly important roles. The decisive turning point from the feudal to the capitalist mode of production was the foundation of the first city-states in Europe. In these cities a large surplus of goods was produced, trading increased and consequently the sphere of influence was expanded. The driving force of this new dynamic economy were artisans and merchants, the "bourgeoisie under the regime of feudalism." This gave way to a kinship system, whose members constituted the ruling class of the city-states. During the Renaissance, this new system was visible in many European states. Some parts of the urban bourgeoisie became independent of the aristocracy and attempts were made to constitute preliminary stages of the capitalist system. The oligarchy of late medieval urban societies invested the surplus of their activities to enforce trade, build up a manufacturing system and other more advanced means of production. The process through which the capitalist

[10] Karl Marx, *The Poverty of Philosophy* (1846/47), in *MECW* 6, 174–175.

system was finally established, however, was not a steady one: there were set-backs and periods in which this process decelerated while in others it speeded up.

Capitalist mode of production

The "*capitalist mode of production*" is characterized by enormous economic dynamism and an extreme division of labor. Capitalist production corresponds with the hitherto highest stage of civilization, which will, as Marx stated, only be surpassed by a future communist society. Through capitalist production, society becomes separated into two main classes, which are sharply divided from each other: capitalist bourgeoisie and proletariat, which are, themselves, divided into a many other subclasses. Capitalist production came into being through the invention of new productive forces that automatically gave rise to this new form of economics. Taking the example of British industrialization of the late eighteenth century, Marx states that the conditions that enable the rise of capitalism are the steam engine and spinning machine, and the importation of cotton and other raw materials that were cheaply produced by slaves in overseas territories. The surplus of economic activity is concentrated amongst a very few. This capital is reinvested in the economy and, as a consequence, a constantly growing concentration of wealth and possessions in the hands of the capitalists: this process is called the *accumulation of capital*. As a consequence of this, the surplus of economic activities is steadily withdrawn from the proletariat. Because of this visible tendency, Marx predicted a growing conflict between these two main classes, which would end in the collapse of capitalist economics. The next stage would be a mode of production in which no private ownership of means of production would be allowed. The economy would be regulated by central governance. Marxism is an optimistic philosophy: civilization begins at a primitive stage, but it automatically evolves further, since man can build his work upon the work of former generations.

1.2. CLASS THEORY

Marx's economic theory is firmly connected with his class theory, which can be understood as a model that describes the social structure of industrialized societies until present times. While many theories conceived by Marx are the object of profound studies in the Western countries, his class theory in particular is explained in a somewhat obscure manner. This might be due to several reasons. One of them is the problem of translating Marx's sociological terms into other European languages. In some cases, Marx's German words have no exact equivalent in English. Thus, the semantics of

Semantics of the term "class"

the German term *Klasse*, which is not identical to "social class." Marx's use of this word is near to today's sense of the term "caste." In German, the word *Klasse* belongs exclusively to Marxist terminology and does not form part of common language. Nevertheless, in this manual, *Klasse* is translated as "class," but in the proper Marxist sense and not as synonym for "social stratum."

Class consciosness and class interest

The members of a class show similar behavior, even when direct communication between them is not possible due to their high number. In relation to this, Marx speaks of "social consciousness" and "class consciousness," which implies the same will to defend the "class interest" (*Klasseninteresse*). To understand why and how this general consciousness of a class is established and how "class" in a Marxist sense can be defined, it is necessary to analyze the position of human beings within the economic system. Affiliation to a class is not determined by financial possession, but rather depends on the position of the human being in relation to the means of production.

If we accept that every human being has nearly the same intelligence and working power, the question arises as to why modern industrialized societies have such a rigid system of class assignment. It seems that the social categorization of a human being is already determined at birth. The answer is disarmingly simple: the social position of the human being depends on whether the family possesses means of production or not. If the latter is the case, the human being has to sell his or her labor to someone, who is in possession of means of production (land, tools, etc.). The worker always earns less than his labor is worth: the surplus value is taken by the owner of productive forces. The capital is "stolen labor." Because of *surplus value*, the owner of capital can steadily expand the capital by investing it. The capitalist class succeeds in acquiring capital at an increasingly faster rate. This *accumulation of capital* has a destructive impact on the structure of the whole society, which is divided in two main classes. The great dissimilarity between these two classes results in *class struggle*, or class conflict, which Marx sometimes called *antagonism*.[11] If the explanations of the Marxist class theory are sometimes quite vague, this may well be due to political reasons, but it is also linked to a problem of translation. Thus, it is necessary to use Marx's own expressions to explain his class theory (plate 2).

Surplus value

Class struggle

Society is divided in two main classes: the *bourgeoisie* is the one in possession of the productive forces, and the *proletariat* does not hold any.

Class of the bourgeoisie

The *capitalist class* (or *bourgeoisie)* is divided into various subclasses. In modern Marxist terminology a distinction can be made between industrial capitalists, landowners, finance capitalists and the petty bourgeoisie. For example, landowners can be subdivided again into different subclasses, such as big landowners and small landowners (the peasantry), landowners as producers of raw materials, etc. So, the bourgeoisie displays a very complex structure. Within this class, there are permanent conflicts of a political and

[11] Karl Marx, *A Contribution to the Critique of Political Economy* (Preface) (1859), in *MECW* 29, 263.

Pl. 2 Model of antagonistic class society

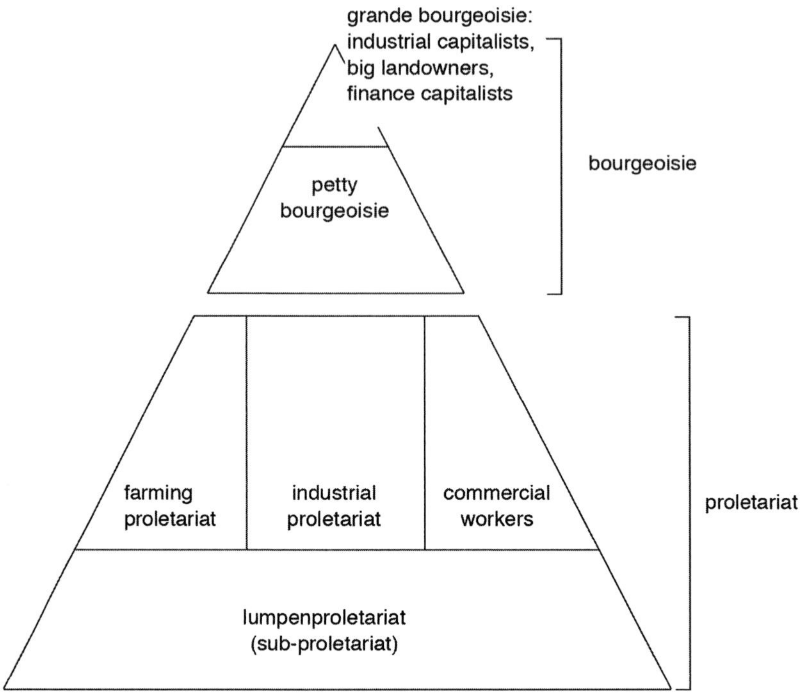

economic nature, which are played out in the public eye and suggest a vivid political life with different factions. But these sometimes very loud and violent conflicts have nothing to do with class struggle, which is more silent and hidden, but is much more effective. These conflicts within the capitalist class are caused by the different relationships of members of the bourgeoisie to the productive forces (for instance, some are in possession of land, whereas others earn their living as merchants). The reason for these conflicts is the striving for a better position of certain productive means against others (for instance, the political struggle for granting subsidies for farmers).

Representing the large majority of the bourgeoisie, the *petty bourgeoisie* (artisans, small merchants and shopkeepers, small peasant proprietors, etc.) occupies a low position in the social order. The petty bourgeoisie possesses means of production only in a very restricted sense. Marx created the term *Mobiliareigentum* (furnishing property) to highlight the small nature of these means. It is not possible for the petty bourgeoisie to accumulate larger stocks of capital: therefore, its position is always insecure. However, this class sees itself firmly bound with the higher class of the larger capital owners, meaning the grande bourgeoisie. It is a general law that those who are at the top of the social pyramid are able to accumulate the capital much quicker than those in lower positions. Marx predicted that accumulation would transfer all capital to the top of society.

Class of the proletariat

The *proletariat* is also subdivided into different classes. The English terms and their German equivalents are: farming proletariat *(Ackerbau-proletariat),* industrial proletariat *(Proletariat)*, commercial workers *(kommerzielle Arbeiter*) and lumpenproletariat (or *sub-proletariat*; the German "*Lumpenproletariat*" is a special sociological term created by Marx). The farming proletariat is not in possession of arable land and agricultural implements. Similarly, the industrial workers operate machinery which is not in their own possession. The commercial workers are identical to today's employees or office workers. An interesting term is "lumpenproletariat," which was adopted as a loan-word in English, but is still a very uncommon term. Its literal translation is "proletariat in shabby clothes," which might fit as a pictorial description even today. The word has another hidden meaning: in German, people referred as to "*Lumpen*" could be described as rogues, rascals or vagabonds. Marx's own translations of this term into English is even more derogatory; he speaks of "the dangerous class" or "the social scum."[12] He avoided having to define this term even though it played a central role in his class theory. But the lumpenproletariat is well described is his *Eighteenth Brumaire of Louis Bonaparte* (1852)[13], where elements of a definition can be derived from different passages. The lumpenproletariat is a very huge class of society that can help a dictator to come to power. It is constituted of people who represent unskilled labor or who have poor education qualifications. As a result, they sometimes have no or only temporary work.[14] Another sociological definition of lumpen-proletariat is that its work is not related to a valuable means of production. Members of this class show no working-class consciousness. In times of crisis, this sub-proletariat[15] can become a revolutionary element, but it is impossible to predict which direction this revolutionary agitation will take. Indeed, the sub-proletariat can support the assumption of power of an extreme right-wing ruler: according to Marx, the dictatorship of Louis Bonaparte was possible through his coalition with the lumpenproletariat.

None of the members of the proletariat are in possession of means of production, and it is impossible for the working class to save enough to acquire capital. The capitalist mode of production yields bad results for this class: the economic crises of capitalism destroy its financial basis in a

[12] Karl Marx and Friedrich Engels, *Manifesto* (1848), in *MECW* 6, 494.

[13] Karl Marx, *The Eighteenth Brumaire of Louis Bonaparte* (1852, according to 1869 ed.), in *MECW* 11, 110, 148–149 (here with satirical definition), 155, 182.

[14] Karl Marx, *Capital,* vol. 1 (1887), in *MECW* 35, 637–638.

[15] The term "lumpenproletariat" corresponds exactly to "sub-proletariat," since Marx means a class that is "under" the classes that are steadily working and earning wages.

recurring rhythm. As a result of capitalist economics and its regular crises, there are a few at the top who have accumulated all capital, and a huge mass without possessions.

Semantics of *bourgeoisie* and the German term *Bürgertum*

The semantics of the term "bourgeoisie" in Marxist texts is not exactly identical to its common sense in French. Marx adopted the word "bourgeoisie" from the French and used it in his writings in German, but he gave it a particular meaning to define the bourgeoisie as the class in possession of the means of production.

When Marx refers to the German word "*Bürgertum*", he did not modify its sense. The modern German word originates in a term which is similar to the English "burgher," which simply means "inhabitants of the medieval urban centers." In the nineteenth century, like today, the word "*Bürgertum*" is a synonym of "citizen." Therefore, "*Bürger*" and "*Bürgertum*" absolutely do not have a relationship with the Marxists theory of classes. In modern German, "*Bürgertum*" includes all classes, except the extreme bottom and top of the social pyramid. Therefore, it has no meaning in modern sociological language and is avoided. In contrast to this, Marx's use of the word "*Bourgeoisie*" (written here with a capital) in his writings in German is well-defined. In German, it is a loan-word from French, and refers exclusively to Marxist terminology, accordingly it is avoided in spoken language. In French as well as in English, the two different German words "*Bourgeoisie*" and "*Bürgertum*" are both translated as "bourgeoisie" (seldom, in English sometimes even as "middle class"), and this effaces the differences between these two terms. In Marxist theory of classes, the "bourgeoisie" designates one of the two great classes of the capitalist society.[16]

Marx's "Bourgeoisie" and "*Kleinbürgertum*" ("petty bourgeoisie") never refer to the "middle class," but this error in translation was made by Marx and Engels themselves in some of their writings published in English. The English translation of their *Manifesto* of 1848 includes the expression "middle classes,"[17] but in the German original, the term "*Mittelstände*" ("middle estates") was used.[18] The idea of a "middle class" is alien to Marx's considerations on an industrial society strictly split into two antagonistic fractions.

Definition of "class" as a Marxist term

The crucial point of Marxist class theory is that the social position of the human beings is defined by their relation to the means of production. In contrast to this, other aspects of assigning a human being to a certain class (such as income, education, etc.) are not regarded as decisive factors. An

---

[16] "*Haute bourgeoisie*" and its German equivalent "*Großbürgertum*" are not Marxist terms. They have a common meaning.

[17] It was not possible for the author of this book to see the original print in English language of 1848, but the text in *MECW* seems to be based on the original edition. Karl Marx and Friedrich Engels, *Manifesto* (1848), in *MECW* 6, 494, note b.

[18] Karl Marx, Friedrich Engels, *Manifest der Kommunistischen Partei* (Stuttgart: Reclam, 1999), 49.

example: the wages and wealth of someone in the working class could be much higher than those of someone in the petty bourgeoisie. But this does not count in Marx's class theory: it is neither the consciousness or the self-assessment of the individual, nor wealth, prestige or other factors, but rather it is the ownership of means of production that defines the affiliation to a certain class. This is it what makes Marxist thought a modern model which is always operational.

Definition of the caste system

The class model described here was developed by an analysis of industrialized societies, but Marx also wrote about the structure of society during historical epochs as well as those in other cultures, in particular what is called the "*caste system.*" If the main social groups of a society are compressed to castes, religious, race-related and other factors prevent even individual members from moving from one caste to another.[19] The caste system causes society's structure as a whole to freeze, and it prevents the further evolution of economics, since the human being has no chance of obtaining a higher social position based on his or her working ability.[20] In contrast to this, classes in a capitalist society are in constant competition with each other. It is almost impossible for the individual to change class, but classes as a whole are evolving as a result of the further development of productive forces or progression in economics.

Changes in the positioning of classes

Marx interpreted social classes as dynamic constructs, which develop in reaction to economic changes, but the affiliation of an individual to a certain class is nearly definitive. Consciousness of the existence of this kind of classes is a central axiom of Marxist sciences. What is termed "class" in most directions of modern sociology is closer to the notion of a "social stratum." The term "class" is quite controversial in English, and several definitions have been offered, but none are universally accepted. Notions of a "social stratum" or of a "middle class" are alien to Marxist philosophy. Unconsciously, human beings act in keeping with the interests of their own class. Classes are not a conscious order of the human mind; they are a consequence of a certain mode of production. The order of society is based on the development of tools and means of production.

[19] Karl Marx, *Capital*, vol. 1 (1887), in *MECW* 35, 362–364.

[20] Therefore, British rule in India was interpreted as a positive matter, since the introduction of a capitalist economy destroyed the old caste-structures. Karl Marx, "The Future of British Rule in India," *New-York Daily Tribune*, August 8, 1853, no. 3840, in *MECW* 12, 217–222.

1.3. HISTORICAL MATERIALISM

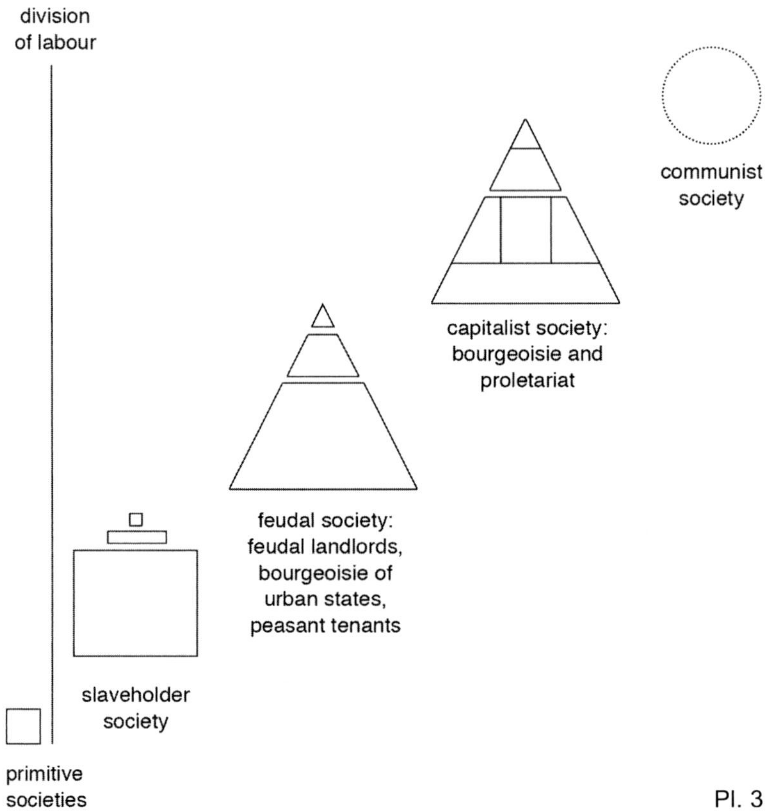

Pl. 3

Marx's conception of history is called historical materialism (plate 3), which stands in accordance with his other principal theories, such as his economic theory and his theory on the evolution of classes. The different stages of this evolution can be summarized in this way: in prehistoric and primitive societies, all individuals assume almost the same social position. Marx talks of a classless society, since means of production are non-existent or unnecessary. However, the formation of classes already began at an early stage of human history. The first civilizations are already characterized by the

Prehistoric and primitive societies

invention of *division of labor*. Marx explained this through the fact that arable land must have been exploited more intensively to satisfy the needs caused by the growth of population: the ancient working methods were not sufficient enough and a specialization into different professions became necessary. This resulted in a division of labor into different professions, such as farmers, hunters, artisans and warriors. Finally, a division into separated social groups became necessary, since even this primitive state of productive techniques gave rise to this.[21]

Slaveholder society

The first advanced civilizations were *slaveholder societies*, which signalizes a primitive stage of productive forces. The achievements of the ancient world are based on the labor of slaves. The ancient mode of production corresponds with a little developed stage of civilization. If in ancient Greece the intellectual and scientific ideas were created that became the starting point of modern civilization, the large majority of the population in conditions not far off from absolutely inhumane. The great cultural achievements of antiquity were conceived in a very small circle belonging to the dominant class whose power was based on a rigid oppression of the masses.

Feudal society

In the Middle Ages, during the stage of *feudalism*, a higher stage of civilization was achieved. In this new stage, the human being was removed from direct and implicit dependence on a master. Feudalism was not a product of a shift of consciousness, but it was instead the result of a higher form of economics, which led to demand for higher flexibility and autonomy for every single person. However, the people in feudal societies were still restricted by the "motley feudal ties that bound man to his natural superiors."[22] This expression refers to Marx's idea that under feudalism, the practice of power was toned down and veiled by humanitarian gestures. In the Middle Ages, society reflected the form of a pyramid, with secular and clerical rulers, who came from the class of feudal landlords, at the top. Their power was based on the possession of the most important means of production: arable land.

Another class, the "feudal bourgeoisie," did not exist in the first centuries of the Middle Ages. It slowly came into being with changes in economics caused by a growth of population and the development of commerce. Marx speaks of "medieval burgesses and the small peasant proprietors [who] were the precursors of the modern bourgeoisie."[23] In larger urban centers, a small class of artisans and merchants began to rival the feudal aristocracy and finally seized political power. Nevertheless, this change only affected a very small segment of the population. In the Middle Ages, the large majority of the population was free or semi-free peasants and serfs. Their legal status, even of the serfs, was better than those of slaves in antiquity.

---

[21] Karl Marx and Friedrich Engels, *The German Ideology* (1846/47), in *MECW* 5, 44–45.

[22] Karl Marx and Friedrich Engels, *Manifesto* (1848), in *MECW* 6, 486–487.

[23] Ibid., 509.

Bourgeois-capitalist society

The transformation from feudal estate society to *bourgeois-capitalist society* reaches its first peak with the Reformation and the peasants' wars of the sixteenth century. Finally, after a period beginning in the twelfth century, this process reached a climax with the French Revolution of 1789. There is not *one* social revolution that marks the transmission from one historical stage to another: rather, historical evolution can be understood as a slow process which is accelerated by social revolutions. To understand the Marxist conception of history, it is absolutely necessary to define the term "revolution." Marx interprets a revolution not as a replacement of the ruling class by another, and not as a change of the governmental system, but as changes in relationships between people and the productive forces (for instance, changes in the legal ownership concerning arable land). Marx interpreted the birth of the capitalist system not as a steadily rising process, but as an irregularly ascending line with set-backs, breaks and interruptions.

In capitalist-bourgeois society, the artificial boundaries of feudalism were abolished, which presented an obstacle for the further development of economy. Because of the growth of population, the invention of new techniques and a multitude of other factors, the development of the economy shows a formidable upturn. Society was now clearly divided into two great social groups: the bourgeoisie and the proletariat. Analyzed as a unit, industrial society displays a more complex social structure than any other society before, since the division of labor quickly evolves further. The subdivision of society into two main classes is connected to Marx's thesis of the accumulation of the capital (see economic theory). Because of the creation of modern industries, a bigger concentration of investment capital becomes necessary; as consequence, modern industries produce a larger profit than in former times. This profit is concentrated in the hands of those who are already in possession of the productive forces. Therefore, the two main classes of capitalist society, the bourgeoisie and the proletariat, drift further apart.

At a certain stage of evolution, relationships of production begin to prevent the progressive advancement of the evolution of productive forces. Evolution reaches a turning point. The barriers built by older relationships of production are broken down by a new formation (another structure of society, other laws, etc.) that enables the further development of productive forces. Marx called this new stage the *communist society*, a society without social classes, since he saw the barriers erected by the existence of classes as the main hindrance to the future development of economics. He predicted that a new social order would balance productive forces and relations of production. He predicted that this new social order where the proletariat owned the productive forces would equilibrate the latter as well as the relation of production.

Communist society

Marx interpreted the struggle between the two main classes of society as the motor of human history. The dominant classes want to maintain their position, whereas the lower classes fight for a better one. History is the history of *class struggle*. Marx interpreted human history as a steady ascension of evolution: from primitive stages it reaches more developed stages, synonymous with progress in freedom and humanity. So, historical materialism is an optimistic vision of human history.

1.4. BASE AND SUPERSTRUCTURE

This theory refers to intellectual work outside the sphere of material production. Whereas a majority of human beings are involved in activities within the economic sphere, there are others who create models of explanation for the whole society. The productive forces and relations of production are the real basis over which a superstructure exists. The function of this superstructure is the production of ideology (plate 4). Since the human being cannot freely choose his or her position in society, he or she cannot escape the ideology produced by the superstructure. Since the superstructure is determined by the modes of production of material life, the producers of ideology are not able to reflect upon the real nature of their mental products.

Obviously, politicians, jurists, clericals and others are in a privileged position and are not involved in the sphere of material production. Within the antagonistic class structure of modern society, very few members of the bourgeoisie are connected with the superstructure, where philosophical, religious, political and legal opinions are produced. The function of the superstructure is to produce illusions:

> The ideas of the ruling class are in every epoch the ruling ideas: i. e., the class which is the ruling *material* force of society is at the same time its ruling *intellectual* force. The class which has the means of material production at its disposal, consequently also controls the means of mental production, so that the ideas of those who lack the means of mental production are on the whole subject to it. The ruling ideas are nothing more than the ideal expression of the dominant material relations. . . .
> [following section:] The division of labor . . . manifests itself also in the ruling class as the division of mental and material labor, so that inside this class one part appears as the thinkers of this class (its active, conceptive ideologists, who make the formation of the illusion of this class about itself to their chief source of livelihood), while the others' attitude to these ideas and illusions are more passive and receptive, because they are in reality the active members of this class and have less time to make up illusions and ideas about themselves.[24]

Pl. 4 Base and superstructure

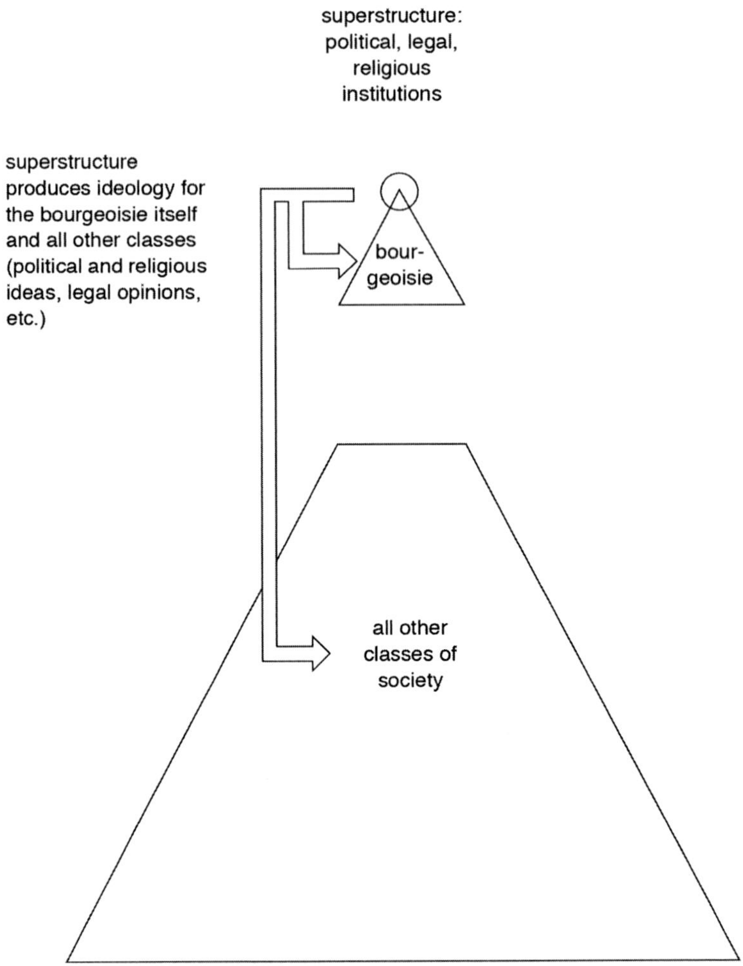

Superstructure is defined by this function within society. Its aim is to produce models for explaining the world, justification of state power, etc. It translates the respective economics and type of rule into an ideology that molds the consciousness of all members of society. Artistic professions do not belong to the superstructure, even when this was suggested by writings of Engels. The superstructure is a supra-individual structure, which changes permanently according to the economic situation and the system of communication. The dominant ideology is produced by relatively small groups, among them are, for instance, the supervisory boards and the directors of large television channels. It is obvious that "art" is only a means of transmission of ideology to the whole society, even though the artist is in no way part of the superstructure. The idea that art is a subconscious product of the means and relations of production has exercised a profound influence on Marxist art history as well as the sociology of art.

2. INTRODUCTION TO MARXIST ART HISTORY

•

There are few remarks in secondary literature on Marxist art theory and history.[1] The following short overview refers in the first chapter not only to Marxist literature, but also to studies related to other directions of socialist thought. Since the extent of Marxist writings on visual arts was extremely limited, the evolution of this genre of literature must be understood in relation to other nineteenth-century socialist theories. In the twentieth century, independent Marxist research was only able to develop during short bursts of time. This might be one of the reasons why in Western Europe only a very small number of works have been able to reach a larger public outside academic circles. *Art and the Industrial Revolution* (1947)[2] by Francis D. Klingender is one of these, but it was, without a doubt, Frederick Antal's *Florentine Painting* (1948)[3] that had the greatest influence on art history. However, it becomes difficult to discover traces of this movement in the literature on art history written in the twentieth-first century.

---

1 Frederick Antal, "Remarks on the Method of Art History," *Burlington Magazine* 91 (1949): 49–52, 73–75; Nicos Hadjinicolaou, *Art History and Class Struggle*, 2nd ed. (London: Pluto, 1979); Jonathan Harris, *The New Art History* (London: Routledge, 2001), 63–93; Andrew Hemingway, ed., *Marxism and the History of Art* (London: Pluto, 2006); Andrew Hemingway, "Marxism and Art," *Oxford Bibliographies*, accessed May 27, 2016.

2 Francis D. Klingender, *Art and the Industrial Revolution* (London: N. Carrington, 1947).

3 Frederick Antal, *Florentine Painting and Its Social Background* (London: Routledge, 1948).

2.1. SOCIALIST ART LITERATUR OF THE NINETEENTH CENTURY

The first efforts to establish Marxist art history date back to the 1910s; therefore it is a modern historiographical method. However, its origins stretch far back to the first decades of the nineteenth century, where some central issues such as the social position of the artist and the utility of artistic work were discussed in writings by Claude-Henri de Saint-Simon, Charles Fourier, and other utopian socialists.[4] In *Du principe de l'art et de sa destination sociale* (1865)[5] Joseph-Pierre Proudhon, one of Marx's strongest enemies, elaborated an advanced theory of socialist art. This work, central to the comprehension of early socialist theory on the arts, is a posthumously edited collection of deliberations on aesthetics, partly combined with some scattered notes with thought on the art of the past and present. Proudhonism represents one of the many movements which were opposed to Marxism. Even when Proudhon regarded the material basis of life as the determining factor of human existence, he believed that the human mind could, to a certain degree, act autonomously. Proudhon's art theory displays strong traces of utilitarian thought, which had its origins in the writings of French utopian socialists. There can be no doubt that Proudhon regards art as an instrument of ideological propaganda. On the other hand, he characterizes it as a means of individual freedom. He repeatedly exposed this kind of paradoxical reasoning, since his philosophy consists in reconciling antagonistic theories to form a coherent ensemble. Discussion still surrounds the question of whether Proudhonism is anarchism—as would be Marx's standpoint—or whether it represents one French variant of socialism.

Without *Du principe de l'art*, the whole evolution of all later socialist writings on art cannot be understood. Since Proudhon's considerations on aesthetics are not grounded in economic science, he constantly refers to such ideas like the soul of the individual, beauty, and freedom of art, appealing with this to the feelings and emotions of the readers, and thus evoked certain interest from artists. In contrast to this, the theory of Marx, mainly exposing a purely economic perspective, had no bearing on artists' thoughts and, consequently, did not leave any traces in their writings.

Socialist art theory has its origins in the French-speaking countries, where it exercised a certain influence on painting and sculpture from the 1830s

[4] Neil McWilliam, *Dreams of Happiness: Social Art and the French Left, 1830–1850* (Princeton: Princeton University Press, 1993).

[5] Pierre-Joseph Proudhon, *Du principe de l'art et de sa destination sociale* (Paris: Garnier Frères, 1865).

onwards. This influence reached a first peak with Courbet's realism from 1850–1851 onwards and a second one in the years shortly after 1880 when a socio-critical variant of naturalism in painting was discussed for a short period of time. It seems that the most remarkable efforts to create a new social art were made in Belgium, where some artists, such as Constantin Meunier, were even termed "socialist artists" or "revolutionary artists."

Reviews by Engels on painting

From the late 1840s onwards, Marxism was only one very small movement among many different competing directions of socialism and fought a ferocious battle for survival. Therefore, considerations on fine arts play a minor role in Marx's and Engels' writings. A Marxist theory especially adapted to the visual arts has its origin in some reviews by Engels on a direction in German painting of the 1840s called "tendency painting" (*Tendenzmalerei*). The painting *The Silesian Weavers* (1844)[6] by Wilhelm Hübner received a euphoric review from him and he described it as "more effectual socialist agitation than a hundred pamphlets."[7] In general, notes by Marx and Engels on visual arts are rarely found in their writings, since it was the political battle which was of central importance for them. The first anthology with a collection of notes by Marx and Engels on literature and art was edited by Mikhail Lifshits in 1933, fifty years after the death of Marx.[8] At the end of the nineteenth century, only a few Marxist intellectuals had reflected on fine arts. Entertaining hopes of seeing the arrival of a new popular art, the majority of them followed the idea of Marx, who rejected contemporary art as an ideological product of the bourgeoisie and its decadence.

Art criticism of German Marxism

The German followers of Marx had such a radical point of view, since all organizations of social democracy had been prohibited during the Bismarck era. In this respect, the situation was different in comparison with France and England where the political climate was much more liberal. After 1890, there were two tendencies perceptible inside the German Social Democratic Party: orthodox Marxism (also called "new Marxism") and revisionism. Some short essays like "Der Kapitalismus und die Kunst" (1890/91)[9] by Franz Mehring are typical examples of this period. Mehring, one of the great party theoreticians of the SPD, vehemently criticized the art of his time. As a result, it is no wonder that bourgeois intellectuals condemned

---

[6] There are three variants of this painting, which in German is called *Die Weber*. One is exhibited in the Rheinisches Landesmuseum, Bonn.

[7] Friedrich Engels, "Rapid Progress of Communism in Germany" (1844), in *Karl Marx, Frederick Engels on Literature and Art: A Selection of Writings*, ed. Lee Baxandall and Stefan Morawski (London: Pluto, 1973), 105.

[8] An edition in English appeared in the 1930s: Mikhail Lifshits [Lifshitz], ed., *The Philosophy of Art of Karl Marx* (New York: Critics Group, 1938).

[9] Franz Mehring, "Der Kapitalismus und die Kunst," *Die Neue Zeit* 9, no. 2 (1890/91): 649–53, 686–90; also contained in Franz Mehring, *Gesammelte Schriften*, vol. 12 (Berlin: Dietz, 1976), 169–80. This article is a review of the annual Great Berlin Art Exhibition.

this as hostility against fine arts.[10] In this respect, the German discussion showed a different character to that in France, Great Britain, and Belgium where socialist writers showed a much friendlier attitude towards contemporary fine arts.

Convinced that present times were a negative phase of human history, German Marxist intellectuals made several deliberations on the future. A revival of the arts, real modern art, only seemed possible through a radical, revolutionary change in society.[11] The same thought was propagated in Russia. Around 1900, there was no common opinion among German Marxists concerning whether contemporary modern painting could be interpreted as a first positive sign of future popular art or as a reflection of the decadence of the bourgeoisie.

Fabian art theory

Another direction of socialist thought had its origins in Great Britain, where it is connected with authors of the Fabian Society founded in 1883/84. Though disputing the theories conceived by Marx, this circle of intellectuals stood at a distance from Marxism, expecting a progressive change through reforms and not a social revolution. On the other hand, writings by Marx and Engels had been published in English very early on and were better known than in any other country except Germany. Some lectures by William Morris of the late 1870s and 1880s are typical examples of Fabian thought on the arts.[12] Even when there are some similarities to Marx's theories, it is absurd to place Morris in this context. For example, Morris uses the term "alienation" but in a sense that totally contradicts Marx's definition of it. Morris defined it as the distance of the human being from nature and not as the physical exhaustion of the human being under capitalist working conditions. Many of Morris's thoughts originated in the writings of his teacher John Ruskin. Nevertheless, of all writers on art under socialist influence of the nineteenth century, William Morris was the best known. The high regard for the applied arts in socialist art theory has its origins in utilitarianism, but it also has one root in Morris's endeavors to create forms of art that would fit the necessities of all classes.

Relationship of socialists to fine art

Regarding the character of socialist writings on fine arts from the first decades of the nineteenth century until 1910, they concentrated predominantly on the practical application of the arts. Some philosophers did connect certain forms of art with specific social classes. In this respect, some socialist texts were not far from French sociology of art, which is often confused with

[10] Franz Xaver Walter, *Sozialismus und moderne Kunst* (Freiburg: Herder, 1901), 90–102.
[11] Roderich Rudolphi, "Kunst und Proletariat," *Die Neue Zeit* 15(1896/97): 316–17; Leo Berg, "Kunst und Kapitalismus," *Die Zukunft* 32 (1900): 152–61.
[12] William Morris, "The Lesser Arts" (1877), in *Collected Works* (London: Ongmans, 1914), 22: 327; Morris, "Useful Work Versus Useless Toil" (1884), in *Collected Works*, 22: 98–120; Morris, "Art and Socialism" (1884), in *Collected Works*, 23: 192–214.

socialist art theory. Since there were very different strands of socialist thought all over Europe, there are few common denominators. Yet one common thought is surely that early socialists had the impression that the fine arts did not belong to the sphere of socialism and that a new utopian art should be created that would fit the needs of the working class. Sometimes, contemporary fine arts were interpreted as highlighting the decadence of the bourgeoisie.

Before 1914, a theoretical literature on a future art in a socialist state developed in all European countries. Nevertheless, it was left undecided as to what the concrete form or style of this future art should be. Works of fine art that were created under the influence of Marxism did not exist. The influence of French socialist literature, especially of Proudhon's writings, was dominant, whereas the Marxist standpoint was perceptible in the German-speaking countries, Russia, and Northern Italy. After 1890, the social question caused the diffusion of socialist writings among large parts of the population in the great European cities like Milan. Certain socialist writings, among them some by Engels, inspired the Italian painter Giuseppe Pellizza da Volpedo to create his famous painting *Il quarto stato* (The Fourth Estate) (1898–1901).

2.2. MARXIST ART HISTORY IN THE SOVIET UNION

The state ideology of the Soviet Union was called Marxism-Leninism. The exact difference between the Marxism of the late nineteenth century and its transformation into Marxism-Leninism is beyond the scope of this work. In short, we can interpret Soviet Marxism of the 1920s as a direct successor of Marx's philosophy, supplemented by theories formulated by Lenin – this fundamentally changed the character of Marxism.

A constant feature which became manifest in writings by socialists reflecting on the arts was a certain distance to the Russian avant-garde of the 1910s. From the end of the 1920s and during the whole Stalinist period this quickly turned into an open hostility against all directions of modern painting. Principally founded on Marx's class theory, this aversion can be explained by the wish to establish an alternative culture based on the traditions of the European workers' movement and opposed to the old bourgeois culture. This new concept of art is already visible in the *Paris Letters* (1913)[13] by Anatoly V. Lunacharsky, who expressed a certain admiration

[13] Anatoly Lunacharsky was the first "Peoples' Commissar for Enlightenment" of the Soviet Union, a position similar to that of a minister of culture and education in the West. Under Lenin

for cubism and other directions of modern painting, but at the same time showed a degree of detachment to these new artistic forms by reducing the art of the avant-garde to a pure experimentation with artistic forms empty of any social content – and without any sense.

Marxist exhibitions in Soviet museums

It might be an unfamiliar idea that a new historiographical method presents itself for the first time in museum exhibitions, but this is exactly what happened when Marxist art history came into being after the October Revolution. The first Marxist exhibition was in the archaeological museum in Khersones, the ancient Chersonesus, in around 1924/25.[14] In the course of the following years, some departments of the great museums in Leningrad and Moscow were reorganized. The characteristic feature of these exhibitions was large panels with explanatory texts. The Russian expression for this kind of museum translates as *talking museum* or *self-explaining museum*.[15]

General conception of Marxist exhibitions

The new museum conceptions evolved very quickly after the revolution, caused by the will to propagate the new state ideology to the masses. Large groups of visitors were led through these exhibitions and listened to explanations by museum guides. The report *On Museums of the Soviet Union* (1932) by the Hungarian art historian Frederick Antal gives an impression of these exhibitions (document 2).[16] It is reasonable to suspect that this new idea of the art museum was conceived by the first generation of Marxist art historians and archaeologists, for instance Fedir Šmit, (transliterated into French as "Théodore Schmit") and Kostjatin Grinevich (German transcription as "Grinewitsch").

The chronological order, choice of art objects, and corresponding comments have their origins in historical materialism, especially in the *Capital* which had been translated into Russian long before the October Revolution. The large number of explanatory panels and the exhibition of objects that did not belong to the sphere of high art was a radical change. A

he took a liberal standpoint. His reviews on exhibitions of modern French painting written in 1913, the *Paris Letters*, were printed in the magazines *Ssowremennik* (The Contemporary) 6 (1913) and *Teatr i iskusstwo* (Theatre and Art) 15 (1913). The German translation is contained in A. Lunacharski, *Die Revolution und die Kunst*, 2nd ed. (Dresden: Verlag der Kunst, 1974), 69–93.

[14] Chersonesus is the name of an ancient city founded by the Greeks on the Crimean Peninsula, near today's Sevastopol. It became a center of Russian archeology during the nineteenth and twentieth centuries. Kostjatin Grinewitsch [Grinevich], "Probleme der Museenexposition in der USSR," in *Museumsgeschichte. Kommentierte Quellentexte 1750–1950*, ed. Kristina Kratz-Kessemeier (Berlin: Reimer, 2010), 266–75 (271); originally published in *Illustrierte Monatsschrift. Organ der Gesellschaft für Kulturelle Verbindung (VOKS)* 2, no. 10–12 (1931): 145–51.

[15] The expression *selbstsprechendes Museum* (self-explaining museum) appeared in an article by the Russian archeologist Grinevich in a German magazine published in 1931, reprinted in Kratz-Kessemeier, *Museumsgeschichte*, 267 (see previous note).

[16] At the time of his visit to the Soviet Union, Antal lived in Berlin. His eyewitness report was written in German and was first published in *Kritische Berichte* 4, no. 2/3 (1976): 5–11.

typical example is Antal's description of the presentation of French art of the Renaissance in the Hermitage in Petrograd:

> The first exhibition room hosts the two main forces of the sixteenth century: knights and peasants. A knight in a mighty suit of armor sits on his horse in the middle of the hall. High up on the wall, a tremendous castle, below it the semi-plastic figure of a bent peasant cultivating the soil. Beside him, quotations of folk songs from this time, laments of the folk.
>
> On a smaller wall, there are tables detailing the division of classes in the sixteenth century, state finances, devaluation of wages. Quotations from Marx and Engels regarding this time and its classes. Citations from speeches of the third estate. In other exhibition halls, the thesis and antithesis of aristocratic and burgher art is displayed through pictures, drawings, arts and crafts.[17]

The new exhibitions of the early Soviet Union radically broke with all traditions of museums in the bourgeois states, not only because of the uncommon commentaries of the exposed objects. The idea of the "high art museum" was abolished. The minor role of painting and sculpture, and strong emphasis on graphic art (drawings, prints, book illustrations, etc.) and arts and crafts objects (ceramic, pottery, weaponry, etc.), supplemented by photographs of architecture, radically brought an end to the old hierarchies.

The categorization of art objects to certain social classes, often realized as a contrast between the ruling class and its competing, upcoming class, is a unique phenomenon in the history of museums. The ordering category of style was still valid, but "style" was interpreted as an unconscious reflection of class ideology. From the early Renaissance onwards, a main contrast was established between aristocratic art and feudal bourgeois art. Later, in the age of early industrialization, the class structure became more complex. Therefore, the epoch-dominating style was subdivided into several class-related styles. The division of nineteenth-century French art in the Hermitage exactly followed the writings of Marx regarding the revolutions of 1830 and 1848 and their related economic, political, and sociological consequences.

The new exhibition systems of Soviet art museums and with them, the new Marxist art history, seem to have sprung out of nowhere, without any

[17] "Im ersten Raum die zwei Hauptkräfte des 16. Jahrhunderts: Ritter und Bauer. Der Ritter im mächtigen Harnisch auf dem Pferde sitzend, in der Mitte des Saales. An der Wand hoch oben eine gewaltige Burg, unter ihr die halb plastische Figur eines gekrümmten, den Boden bearbeitenden Bauern. Neben ihm Zitate aus Volksliedern der Zeit, Klagelieder des Volkes.

An einer kleineren Wand Tabellen betreffs Verteilung der Klassen im 16. Jahrhundert, die staatlichen Finanzen, die Devaluation des Lohnes. Zitate aus Marx und Engels, diese Zeit und diese Klassen betreffend. Zitate aus Reden des dritten Standes. In den weiteren Sälen die These und Antithese von adliger und bürgerlicher Kunst durchgeführt, durchgeführt an Bildern, Zeichnungen, Kunstgewerbe." Frederick Antal, "Über Museen in der Sowjetunion" (1932), *Kritische Berichte* 4, no. 2/3 (1976): 5.

precursors. Certainly, nineteenth-century socialist art literature was one source, but it had a purely utopian-theoretical character and had not developed an art historical ordering system. Bourgeois nineteenth-century art history could have been a reference point, but English and German art history exposed a purely idealistic character that constitutes the exact counterposition to Marxism.

French art literature of the nineteenth century as a point of reference

If Antal's description is examined word for word, a main source can be specified: for instance, he mentions the contrast between painting in rococo style (Boucher, Fragonard) and the painters inspired by the Enlightenment (Chardin, Greuze, Hallé); furthermore, French political-satirical graphic art and caricature (Daumier, Gavarni) and French Proto-Realism of the 1840s (Béranger). This deep knowledge of socio-critical directions in French art leads one to assume that young Soviet art historians were largely influenced by French authors belonging to the liberal bourgeoisie. This latter group had already established a link between works of high art and certain social classes. French art literature of the nineteenth century seems to have inspired Soviet art history. To mention one example, one source could have been *Histoire de la caricature* (1865–1888) by Champfleury. It is a mostly unknown fact that there had been translations of French art literature, for instance of Proudhon's *Du principle de l'art.*[18] In the nineteenth century and in the first decades of the twentieth century, like in other European countries, French was the *lingua franca* of Russian intellectuals. Additionally, Russian libraries contained many books by French left-wing authors such as *L'art au point de vue sociologique* (1889) by Jean-Marie Guyau and the *Essais socialistes* (1906) by Emile Vandervelde. It can be taken as a certain fact that Russian intellectuals were familiar with the French discussion on social art and realism in painting and literature.

"Realism" im early Marxist literature

This explains that realism as a central conception of all arts was propagated by the revolutionary government in the 1920s. In the writings of Marx, realism in literature played a subordinated role; he attributed it to the liberal bourgeois culture, which, in fact, it really was during his lifetime. It was not until 1885[19] or 1888[20] that Engels undertook a deeper analysis of realism in literature. After 1917, the debate on realism was relatively new among Soviet Marxist theoreticians, but they quickly adopted the subject and transferred it to their own theories. However, in early Marxist exhibitions, categorization regarding "realism" and "bourgeois art" did not play a significant role. The priority was the visualization of the context between "style" and "class consciousness."

[18] Pierre-Joseph Proudhon, [Art, Its Principles and Public Purposes] (St Petersburg: 1895).

[19] The first comment is in a letter from Engels to Minna Kautsky, dated 26 November 1885, in Karl Marx und Friedrich Engels, *Über Kunst und Literatur* (Berlin: Dietz, 1967), 1: 156.

[20] Letter from F. Engels to Margaret Harkness, dated April 1888, in *Karl Marx, Frederick Engels on Literature and Art* (London: Pluto 1973), 116.

First principles of Marxist art history

In the 1920s, Soviet art historians realized that "style" was connected with the ideology of the class that gave commissions to artists. Consequently, a change of one ideology to another is even visible in the works of individual artists. For instance, the work of graphic artists of the late feudal era can be subdivided into the categories "aristocratic" and "popular." A change is also visible in the development of certain styles: the style of classicism oscillated several times between the poles "progressive" and "reactionary." The classicism carried by progressive classes, for instance during the French Revolution, has a different character to that of the Restoration epochs. This model can be adopted for all other forms of artistic expression.

Marxist art theory

The hypothesis can be made that the early Marxist exhibitions of the 1920s already reflected the structure of later Soviet art historical literature. Unfortunately, there were no translations of Soviet art histories from the 1920s to the mid-1950s into English and German. Caused by the isolation of the Soviet Union, only a few Russian books of this period are available in Western European libraries. The only exceptions are the publications by Mikhail Lifshits, the leading philosopher on Marxist art theory with an international reputation. Very little was known until the 1930s about Marx's and Engels's statements on fine arts, but in 1933, Lifshits published a small manual containing essential passages on art theory taken from books, manuscripts, letters and other texts by Marx and Engels. In 1938, this volume was published in English, but already in 1936 a French anthology had appeared that was mostly independent of Lifshits' work.[21] In the years 1967 and 1968, an anthology in German was published that might be the most expanded version.[22] A Spanish edition based on the French edition of 1936 appeared in 1965 and 1972.[23] There are three different Italian anthologies of the works by Marx and Engels on art and literature, of which the one by Carlo Salinari seems to be the best-known. There are also two different anthologies in Portuguese, one of which was published in 2010 in Brazil – this latter work has absolutely nothing in common with Lifshits' anthology of 1933, for it represents a new line of development.[24]

---

[21] Mikhail Lifshits, *The Philosophy of Art of Karl Marx* (New York: Critics Group, 1938). Karl Marx and Friedrich Engels (Jean Fréville, ed.), *Sur la littérature et l'art* (Paris: Éditions sociales internationales, 1936).

[22] Karl Marx and Friedrich Engels, *Über Kunst und Literatur,* 2 vols. (Berlin: Dietz, 1967/68)

[23] Carlos Marx and Federico Engels, *Sobre la literatura y el arte* (La Habana: Instituto Cubano del Libro, 1965).

[24] [Italian editions:] Karl Marx and Friedrich Engels (Valentino Gerratana, ed.), *Sull'arte e la letteratura* (Milano, Novarra: Cooperativa del Libro Popolare, 1954); Karl Marx and Friedrich Engels (Carlo Salinari, ed.), *Scritti sull'arte* (Rome: Laterza, 1967); Karl Marx (Giuseppe Prestipino, ed.), *Arte e lavoro: scritti di estetica* (Rome: Newton Compton, 1976). [Portuguese editions:] Karl Marx and Friedrich Engels, *Sobre literatura e arte* (Lisbon: Estampa, 1971); Karl Marx and Friedrich Engels: *Cultura, arte e literatura – textos escolhidos* (São Paulo: Expressão popular, 2010).

Soviet art history of the 1950s

During the 1950s, when the first German translations of Russian art historical books appeared, it became obvious that these books had a very different character compared to those of Soviet Marxism of the 1920s. This new character can be described as "superficial Marxism" or "vulgar Marxism", which means a simplified interpretation of Marxism. These books differ to a large extent from the point of view exposed in the exhibitions in art museums in the Soviet Union of the 1920s. From the late 1930s onwards, Marxism became an instrument of totalitarian rule. It was also the process of bureaucratization that changed Marxism into a stiff doctrine. However, this version of the evolution of Soviet Marxism, propagated during the twentieth century in the West seems to be too simple, for the evolution had been much more complex.

The General History of Art (1956–1966)[25] is a typical example of Soviet art history. This large research project, the most important regarding art history of the Soviet era, was translated into German as *Allgemeine Geschichte der Kunst* (1961–1972).[26] This *General History of Art* has largely a non-Marxist character, even when superficial Marxist rhetoric is evident in all volumes. Even when every volume opens with a short historical summary of each epoch interpreted from the Marxist-Leninist point of view, the texts in their entirety are marked by a historiography with a strong conservative stamp. For instance, the fourth volume on the art of the Renaissance reflects the traditional structure established by bourgeois art history of the nineteenth century. This volume displays a sort of history writing viewed from an idealizing standpoint partly with surprisingly strong romanticizing features. Even the publications by Antal on the Italian Renaissance are absent.[27] The same idealizing character can be seen in the eighth volume on art in the socialist countries of the twentieth century that represents resolutely idealizing and non-critical point of view. On the other hand, the seventh volume on the art of the twentieth century in capitalist countries shows a tendency towards Marxist criticism. This volume is still a good source regarding socio-critical tendencies that penetrated painting and graphic art in the West until the end of the 1950s[28], but even here the analysis seems to be a clever dodge, since this sort of criticism was strongly encouraged by official Soviet directives.

[25] Academy of Arts of the USSR, Institute of Theory and History of Fine Arts, [General History of the Arts], ed. B. V. Veimarn et al. (Moscow: Iskusstvo, 1956-1966).

[26] Akademie der Künste der UDSSR, *Allgemeine Geschichte der Kunst*, 8 vols., ed. B. V. Veimarn et al., editior of the German translation Ullrich Kuhirt (Leipzig: Seemann, 1961–1972).

[27] See the Renaissance volume *Allgemeine Geschichte der Kunst*, vol. 4, *Die Kunst der Renaissancezeit* (Leipzig: Seemann, 1965).

[28] Akademie der Künste der UDSSR, *Allgemeine Geschichte der Kunst*, vol. 7, *Die Kunst des 20. Jahrhunderts* (Leipzig: Seemann, 1969).

There is no simple answer to the question of what happened to Marxist art history in the years after 1930. When Soviet socialism collapsed in the year 1990, it seems that there was no Marxist school of art history at Russian universities. However, the Marxist analysis influenced other branches of Soviet social sciences, for instance political historiography. In the field of art history, there had been a multitude of different factors, such as bureaucratization and the simplification of Marxist philosophy from the 1930s onwards that turned Russian art history in the conservative direction. There can be no doubt that Marxism became a dead formula for many people.

2.3. WESTERN MARXIST ART HISTORY

O

It was not until the 1930s that Western Marxist history came into being. Factors that caused the acceptance of this method were the world economic crisis and the subsequent dominance of totalitarian states in Europe. Many art historians of Jewish origin, such as Antal, Hauser, and Raphael, were forced to live in exile. The emergence of scientific Marxism was favored by several circumstances, such as the importance of a workers' movement and the existence of a socialist press in Central Europe before the dominion of fascism. Marxists intellectuals and organized workers were convinced that a state based on the principles of socialism had been erected in Russia, and this might have encouraged their political activities, including in the field of art.

Classic writers of Marxist art history

Regarding the period from the 1930s to the 1960s, we cannot speak of a "school" but rather only of more or less isolated writers of Marxist art history. Those still known today are Frederick Antal, Francis Donald Klingender, Meyer Schapiro, and Max Raphael.

Florentine Painting (1948)[29] by Antal has to be regarded as a pioneering work.[30] The origins of this book lie in a research project of the 1930s. His second main work is *Hogarth and His Place in European Art* (1962).[31] Other posthumously published manuscripts are highly problematic. It is obvious that the author never intended these drafts to be published.[32] The

[29] Frederick Antal, *Florentine Painting.*

[30] On Antal, see *Kritische Berichte* 4, no. 2/3 (1976) and Paul Stirton, "Frederick Antal," in Hemingway, *Marxism and the History of Art*, 45–66.

[31] Frederick Antal, *Hogarth and His Place in European Art* (London: Routledge & Kegan Paul, 1962).

[32] For instance *Raffael zwischen Renaissance and Romantik. Eine sozialgeschichtliche Einführung in die mittelitalienische Malerei des 16. und 17. Jahrhunderts* (Giessen: Anabas, 1980).

origins of Marxist art history in the West are described in Antal's article "On the Method of Art History" (1949).[33] The efforts of English historians to create a "social history" in the 1940s are recognized to have caused a similar tendency within the field of art history.

It is remarkable that this article does not contain the word "Marxism", which was taboo then. As precursors, he mentions the Vienna school of art history and the efforts of Aby Warburg to position art history within a larger cultural context. Antal lists only a few books that were close to his method. Besides *Artistic Theory in Italy 1450–1600* (1940) by Anthony Blunt, he refers to Meyer Schapiro.

The publications by Francis D. Klingender are the only texts written by a Marxist art historian that have reached a larger public. His main work *Art and the Industrial Revolution* (1947)[34] served as an accompanying text to an exhibition whose theme was the early history of industrialization in Great Britain in the eighteen and nineteenth centuries. He also published *Goya in the Democratic Tradition* (1948),[35] which might be the first Marxist biography of a painter in the West. Since Marx regarded the individual as guided by subordinated class interests, there were consequently no efforts made by Marxist historians to write about the lives of individual painters and sculptors. In *Goya*, this methodological problem is solved by using the individual life of an artist as an example to explain the social and political situation of a certain epoch.

An interesting position is adopted by Meyer Schapiro, who is sometimes regarded as one of the most important Marxist art historians of the twentieth century.[36] This assessment seems to be irritating at first: he neither used Marxist terminology, nor did he include social or political comments in his writings. Among other things, this stems from his specific method. He documented his research work in scientific articles; the most important of these are collected in *Selected Papers* (1977–1999).[37] The great merit of Schapiro is his assertion of unfamiliar theses that enrich several special fields of art history. Yet, seen in retrospect, his different hypotheses have found little acceptance among art historians until the present day.

---

[33] Frederick Antal, "Remarks on the Method of Art History," in *Burlington Magazine* 91 (1949): 49–52, 73–75.

[34] Francis D. Klingender, *Art and the Industrial Revolution*.

[35] Francis D. Klingender, *Goya in the Democratic Tradition* (London: Sidgwick & Jackson, 1948).

[36] Andrew Hemingway, "Meyer Schapiro," *Marxism and the History of Art*, 123–42.

[37] Meyer Schapiro, *Romanesque Art*, Selected Papers 1 (New York: George Braziller, 1977); *Modern Art: 19th and 20th Centuries*, Selected Papers 2 (New York: George Braziller, 1979); *Late Antique, Early Christian and Mediaeval Art*, Selected Papers 3 (New York: George Braziller, 1979); *Theory and Philosophy of Art*, Selected Papers 4 (New York: George Braziller, 1994); *Worldview in Painting: Art and Society*, Selected Papers 5 (New York: George Braziller, 1999).

Stamped by a resolutely philosophical interpretation of Marxism, the writings by Max Raphael belong more to the sphere of theory of art than to art history.[38] During his lifetime, only a few articles and books were printed. The most important is an article entitled *Marx. Zur Kunsttheorie des dialektischen Materialismus*(1932),[39] which had been edited in several versions under different titles. Then, a small booklet appeared, first published in French, entitled *Proudhon, Marx, Picasso* (1933).[40] Another important publication is a posthumously printed anthology of his essays entitled *The Demands of Art* (1968).[41] Since his unpublished manuscriptswere mostly written in German, the posthumous edition projects are in this language: *Arbeiter, Kunst und Künstler* (written 1936–1939; publ. 1975)[42] and the *Werkausgabe* (1983–1987; 1989). There are two different editions of his collected works: the *Campus/Qumran* edition (1983–1987) and the *Suhrkamp* edition (1989).[43]

Sometimes, the free interpretation of Marx's thought by Raphael is extremely problematic. For instance, if we take his interpretation of "myth," we must recognize that the concept of "myth" assumes a very minor role in Marxist philosophy, but was given huge significance by Raphael. He changed the semantics of some central Marxist terms to create an individualistic interpretation of this philosophy. This can be accepted, since a philosophy that is intended to explain and change the contemporary world has to be steadily changed and modernized. But it is doubtful whether the long-winded and complicated thoughts of Raphael did produce a practical art history; he was much closer to art theory. His writings display a monad-like isolation from the outer world, even when some of his drafts appeal to a fictitious audience of "workers". Interest in Raphael dates back to the late 1960s. His free interpretation of Marx's ideas corresponded with the general direction of New Left thought.

---

[38] On his biography, see Stanley Mitchell, "Max Raphael: Aesthetics and Politics," in Hemingway, *Marxism and the History of Art*, 89–105.

[39] Max Raphael, "Marx. Zur Kunsttheorie des dialektischen Materialismus" (On Art Theory of Dialectical Materialism), *Philosophische Hefte* 3 (1932), 125–52. "Dialectical materialism" is a synonym for "Marxism" here.

[40] Max Raphael, *Proudhon, Marx, Picasso: trois études sur la sociologie de l'art* (Paris: Éd. Excelsior, 1933). Translated by Inge Marcuse as *Proudhon, Marx, Picasso: Three Studies in Marxist Aesthetics* (London: Lawrence & Wishart, 1980).

[41] Max Raphael, *The Demands of Art*, ed. John Tagg (Princeton: Princeton University Press, 1968).

[42] Max Raphael, *Arbeiter, Kunst und Künstler* (Frankfurt a. M.: Fischer, 1975).

[43] First edition was *Max Raphael. Kunsttheoretische Schriften* or *Werkausgabe*, ed. Klaus Binder and Hans-Jürgen Heinrich, 8 vols. (Frankfurt a. M.: Campus and Edition Qumran, 1983–1987); second (pocket book) edition was *Max Raphael. Werkausgabe,* ed. Hans-Jürgen Heinrich, 11 vols. (Frankfurt a. M.: Suhrkamp, 1989).

2.4. ACADEMIC MARXISM

The expression "academic Marxism" refers to the observation that a Marxist art history was established for a short period in a few universities in Italy, England, and Germany from 1945 until 1980. Molded with a pronounced academic character, this variant of Marxim began to display features that made it unusable in political practice. The majority of academics did not expect the emergence of a socialist society and, in fact, many intellectuals of the New Left were members of the liberal bourgeoisie. The period from 1968 to the 1970s saw the emergence of very progressive debates, mostly centered towards the liberation of the individual. In the West, this prepared the ground for the dominating philosophies in social sciences in the twenty-first century. Over the course of years, Marxism was overloaded with theories adopted from bourgeois philosophy until its main theories were beyond recognition.

A general overview of Marxist art historical literature in Italy, West Germany, the former German Democratic Republic, England, and, as an example of Marxist art history in developing countries, in the Philippines, will be offered in the next subchapters.

Marxist art history and archaeology in Italy assumed a special role in Europe. Italy
After 1944, the influence of Marxism was strong, since a socialist society became a goal for large parts of the population. The Italian Communist Party (PCI) was the biggest communist organization in the West until 1990. The 1950s represented the climax of Marxist research in the fields of archaeology and art history. One example of this literature is *Organicità e astrazione* (1956)[44] by Ranuccio Bianchi Bandinelli, in which the evolution of two different general directions in visual arts, called "naturalistic" and "abstract," is expounded, beginning with the ancient world until the early Middle Ages. Italian art historians took a different position to their Soviet colleagues. The Italians exposed a certain admiration for modern painting, especially of Picasso's art, since this was interpreted as a symbol of liberation. Taking this into respect, Italian Marxism represented a new level of Marxist interpretation that was better adapted to the cultural context of the post-war era.

Well-known art historians of this epoch are Raffaele de Grada, Corrado Maltese and, as a representative of the younger generation, Antonello Negri. In the field of history of architecture and design, the publications of Giulio Carlo Argan and Manfredo Tafuri reached a large audience. However, it is not possible to mention the many archaeologists, theoreticians, and art

[44] Ranuccio Bianchi Bandinelli, *Organicità e astrazione* (Milano: Feltrinelli, 1956); published in German as *Wirklichkeit und Abstraktion* (Dresden: Verlag der Kunst, 1962).

historians of this direction. There was a well-developed left-wing and communist press in the 1950s that produced a strong echo of their writings. The Italian edition of *Florentine Painting* by Antal received several positive reviews, since his book was regarded as something similar to the efforts of Italian scientists. It is difficult to give an indication of when the Marxist influence on Italian social sciences ended. One turning point was surely the year 1956, in which the Soviet Union suppressed the Hungarian uprising. Furthermore, capitalism began to assert its claim on Italian society from the 1950s on.

Nevertheless, the influence of Marxists inside the universities was still strong. Until the 1980s, there were different scientific publications based on Marxist analysis. A typical article is "La periodizzazione della storia dell'arte italiana" (The Chronology of Italian Art History) (1979)[45] by Giovanni Previtali. In this article the traditional division of art periods is critically debated. Previtali examines whether the economic situation really was mirrored in the evolution of the arts, as former Marxist historians have stated. In the end, he comes to the conclusion that there is no "law" regarding the relationship between the economic situation and the evolution of the arts: even if the economic trend is sometimes reflected in the arts, there are many exceptions. In this respect, the article by Previtali is a typical example of Marxism of this epoch: the theories established by former Marxist historians were critically reconsidered to elaborate a new sort of historiography with strong intellectual features. During the 1970s, the ideas of May 1968 in France and of the New Left in the English-speaking countries influenced the political discourse inside the universities.

German Democratic Republic

A highly developed Marxist art literature existed in the German Democratic Republic (GDR) between 1949 and 1990. Especially in the period stretching from 1950 until 1960, it was intended to establish Marxism as an analytical instrument of social sciences. The first generation of art historians of the GDR had been eyewitnesses to world economic crises, the collapse of the Weimar Republic, and the suffering of socialists and communists under Nazi dictatorship. Therefore, early GDR literature has a definite anti-fascist character, which continues to make some parts of it convincing even today.

A main emphasis of early German Marxist art history was research on German Renaissance art. A pattern for sociological analysis had been established long before, with *Peasant War* (1850) by Friedrich Engels. A typical work of early GDR literature is *Lucas Cranach* (1953)[46] by Heinz

---

[45] Giovanni Previtali, "La periodizzazione della storia dell'arte italiana," in *Storia dell'arte italiana*, ed. Giulio Bollati and Paolo Fossati, 1st part, vol. 1 (Torino: G. Einaudi, 1979–1983): 3–96.

[46] Heinz Lüdecke, *Lucas Cranach der Ältere. Der Künstler und seine Zeit* (Berlin: Henschelverlag, 1953); see especially the chapter on Cranach, 99–127.

Lüdecke. Other examples are the biography *Jörg Ratgeb* (1972)[47] by Wilhelm Fraenger and *Die drei gottlosen Maler von Nürnberg* (The Three Godless Painters of Nuremberg) (1975)[48] by Herbert Zschelletzschky. At the time of their publication, these books were vehemently criticized or ignored in the West, and some still are even today. The book by Zschelletzschky is one of the few examples of an expanded art history according to the Marxist-Leninist method in German—and it is, perhaps, the most interesting. Published in the mid-1970s, when Marxist methods already showed strong signs of decline in the socialist countries, the book is reminiscent of the 1950s. The dogmatic Marxism exposed there is not typical of GDR art literature. The author describes in detail the biographies and artistic work of Sebald Beham, Barthel Beham, and Georg Pencz. Since these artists belonged to the sect of Thomas Münzer,[49] they were interpreted to be the forerunners of political radical artists. Zschelletzschky attempted to establish a Marxist iconography by analyzing the pictorial elements of graphic series of the Renaissance. Even if sometimes convincing, these interpretation are strongly rejected today.

A series of pocket books entitled *Fundus-Bücher*[50] contains some works based on the Marxist method (V. Gordon Childe, Georg Lukács, Mikhail Lifshits, Sidney Finkelstein, and translations of Russian and other East European authors of the 1950s and 1960s). The *Fundus* series contained very different genres of scientific literature: theory of literature and art, archaeology, art history, theoretical discussions, biographies of artists and monographs on certain genres of art.

In the years immediately after its foundation, the focus of GDR art literature was on the history of architecture and town planning, book art and typography, and similar fields. Examples are *Idealstädte* (1957)[51] by Georg Münter and *Schriftkunst* (1971)[52] by Albert Kapr. No similar literature has come out of the West to this day.

During the second and last phase of the development of scientific literature, stretching from the mid-1960s to 1989, the Marxist influence on social science of the GDR began to dwindle rapidly, not only in the domain of the fine arts. Art history began to move closer to that in the West, even when the rhetoric of certain passages of art books suggested a "Marxism of the surface." For instance, the well-known book *Düsseldorfer Malerschule* (1964)[53] by Wolfgang Hütt was printed after the end of the GDR in a third

---

[47] Wilhelm Fraenger, *Jörg Ratgeb* (Dresden: Verlag der Kunst, 1972).

[48] H. Zschelletzschky, *Die "Drei gottlosen Maler" von Nürnberg Sebald Beham, Barthel Beham und Georg Pencz* (Leipzig: Seemann, 1975).

[49] Also written as "Müntzer" in German.

[50] Edited by Erhard Frommhold.

[51] Georg Münter, *Idealstädte* (Berlin: Henschelverlag, 1957).

[52] Albert Kapr, *Schriftkunst. Geschichte, Anatomie und Schönheit der lateinischen Buchstaben* (Dresden: Verlag der Kunst, 1971).

[53] Wolfgang Hütt, *Düsseldorfer Malerschule* (Leipzig: Seemann, 1964).

edition with only very slight changes of contents.[54] Another remarkable work is the two volumes on German art from 1890 to 1945 by Harald Olbrich.[55] There are still some signs of the former Marxist method, like the special emphasis on town planning and architecture, and a strong interest in the history of social theories. The most important art historian of the late GDR was Peter H. Feist.

Art history of the late GDR showed a tendency towards a revaluation of Prussian history. In doing this, perhaps, we can detect a mirroring of a similar evolution in the late Soviet Union, with its surprising turn towards an art history that displayed nationalistic features. The myth that was built around the painter Adolph von Menzel, the most popular painter of the German Reich, might be the most astounding example. Driven by a small local patriotism, this painter of the Prussian emperors was regarded as a forerunner of modern realism. His life and works were completely reinterpreted according to this hypothesis, so that Menzel now seemed to be a brave and socially conscious artist and not the obsequious subject that he had been in reality. It was no accident that the Menzel myth was one of the few elements of art history of East Germany was adopted and resumed in West Germany.

Federal Republic of Germany

In the years between 1949 and 1963, it was not possible to establish Marxism inside the universities of the Federal Republic of Germany (FRG), since the era of chancellor Konrad Adenauer was a time of strong oppression of all left-wing tendencies. In the years immediately after 1968, there was a short-lived interest in critical thought.The progressive art history of these years showed a certain relationship to social history of art. Nevertheless, it would not be an objective assessment if the influence of the '68-movement was entirely denied.[56] There were even attempts to constitute free and critical research in the history of literature and art outside the universities. The most prominent example is the *Neue Gesellschaft für Bildende Künste* in West Berlin, which organized several art exhibitions and offered new views on art history in its accompanying catalogues.

A new analysis of Marx's writings is visible in art theoretical publications by Konrad Farner[57] and Thomas Metscher[58]—as abstract theorization reached a certain peak in the 1970s. This neo-Marxism, as it was called in West Germany, cannot be clearly separated from the Frankfurt school of

---

[54] Wolfgang Hütt, *Düsseldorfer Malerschule*, 3rd ed. (Leipzig: Seemann, 1995).

[55] Harald Olbrich, ed., *Geschichte der deutschen Kunst 1890–1918* (Leipzig: Seemann, 1988); Olbrich, ed., *Geschichte der deutschen Kunst 1918–1945* (Leipzig: Seemann, 1990).

[56] The progressive tendency of this time is displayed in the first annual volumes (1973 ff) of the art historical review *Kritische Berichte*, edited by Ulmer Verein.

[57] Konrad Farner, *Kunst als Engagement. Zehn ausgewählte Essays* (Darmstadt: Luchterhand, 1973).

[58] Thomas Metscher, *Kunst und sozialer Prozeß. Studien zu einer Theorie der ästhetischen Erkenntnis* (Cologne: Pahl-Rugenstein, 1977).

Critical Theory. A typical feature of all FRG authors who wrote on art is the absence of Marxist class theory.

Typical art historical works of this period are *Malerei im deutschen Faschismus* (1974)[59] by Berthold Hinz and *Die Villa als Herrschaftsstruktur* (1970)[60] by Reinhard Bentmann and Michael Müller. An author who wrote on architecture and town planning was Thilo Hilpert. A renowned Marxist art historian was Otto Karl Werckmeister, who taught in the United States. His influence in West Germany was insignificant, even if most of his books appeared in English as well as German. An exception is the German edition of *Zitadellenkultur* (1989),[61] which has caused some debate within German universities. The idea that the high culture of the capitalist countries is hermetically isolated from that of lower-class and foreign cultures—for instance of migrants—a notion that had been accepted for a long time in the multiculturally structured English-speaking countries—was seen as an uncommon thought among German academics. Werckmeister's later publications have to be examined very critically, since he tended towards an unstructured mixture of different subject matters.

Aside from neo-Marxism, which only exercised a limited influence during the 1970s and 1980s, the dominant progressive direction was Critical Theory, which has also left some traces in art theory and to a much lesser extent in art history. In the 1970s, the writings of Theodor Adorno and other representatives of the Frankfurt school played a certain role within the academic discussions. Critical Theory has its roots in different social theories of the nineteenth century, in Marxism and in the bourgeois Enlightenment of the eighteenth century.

The last activities regarding Marxism in art literature can be seen in the years between 1990 and 1993 during the liberal phase of the Berlin Republic, when different books that originated in art historical research of the late GDR appeared in print. Most of them were long-term research projects that were finished abruptly and hastily put into print.

Great Britain

Today, Marxism seems to be present in art history practiced in the universities of Great Britain. After the first generation of Marxist art historians, such as Frederick Antal and Francis Klingender, Marxism was transformed into a moderate doctrine that stood in continuation of the Fabian Society of the nineteenth century. German Critical Theory had a certain influence too. In England, it is regarded as a continuation or a modification of Marxism. It

[59] Berthold Hinz, *Die Malerei im deutschen Faschismus. Kunst und Konterrevolution* (Munich: C. Hanser, 1974).

[60] Reinhard Bentmann and Michael Müller, *Die Villa als Herrschaftsstruktur* (Frankurt a. M.: Suhrkamp, 1970).

[61] Otto Karl Werckmeister, *Zitadellenkultur. Die Schöne Kunst des Untergangs in der Kultur der achtziger Jahre*, (Munich: Hanser, 1989). Published in English as *Citadel Culture* (Chicago: Chicago University Press, 1991).

is a special feature of English Marxism to call different directions of left-wing thought Marxism, which are not regarded as such in other countries. This already became obvious in the 1970s with the anthology *Marxism and Art* (1979).[62] Marxism in art theory and history shows a continuation until the present day. A bibliography that reviews Marxist literature (mostly of the English-speaking countries) is the online article "Marxism and Art" (2015)[63] by Andrew Hemingway: here, a great number of publications on art are designated as being "Marxist". In the Anglophone world, the word "Marxism" has a much wider meaning than in other countries and there is the tendency to order works under this label that really do not belong in this category. Even when there is a great number of authors and works, in the following section only a small selection is mentioned.

Even during the Cold War, the academic discussion in Britain had a progressive accent. It was in England that Arnold Hauser created his main works including his *Social History of Art* (1951).[64] In the tradition of French sociology of art, he discusses the evolution of art sciences and the history of literature. Artistic activities are, according to him, guided by several subordinated psychological components that exist independently of society. Nevertheless, Hauser was conscious of the limits of these components within the capitalist system. We can understand the *Social History of Art* as a successful attempt to present a neutral and systematic description of progressive theoretical literature. His book had a great influence on Western humanities during the 1950s and early 1960s, when an extremely strong suppression of all critical endeavors within European universities took place. Belonging to the following generation, Raymond Williams seems to have had a certain influence. His views are the result of a profound study of the writings of Marx and Engels. However, Williams was not an art historian, and he wrote about art and literature from a wider perspective. A new impulse came from the social movements post-2008 in England. *Artists of the Left* (2002)[65] and *The Mysticism of Money* (2013)[66] by Andrew Hemingway stand in continuation of the line of social history of art. Both books describe the tradition of social art in the United States between the 1920s and 1950s.

There is an extensive amount of British literature on art theory. The anthology *Renew Marxist Art History* (2013)[67] gives an overview of this direction in Great Britain. The most important text regarding Marxist art

---

[62] Maynard Solomon, ed., *Marxism and Art* (Brighton: Harvester Press, 1979).

[63] Hemingway, "Marxism and Art," *Oxford Bibliographies*, accessed May 27, 2016.

[64] Arnold Hauser, *The Social History of Art*, 2 vols. (London: Routledge, 1951).

[65] Andrew Hemingway, *Artists on the Left: American Artists and the Communist Movement 1926–1956* (New Haven: Yale University Press, 2002).

[66] Andrew Hemingway, *The Mysticism of Money: Precisionist Painting and Machine Age America* (Pittsburgh: Periscope, 2013).

[67] Warren Carter, Barnaby Haran, and Frederic J. Schwartz, eds., *Renew Marxist Art History* (London: Art Books, 2013).

theory seems to be the preface by John Roberts in his anthology *Art Has No History!* (1994).[68]

Marxist art literature in emergent countries

Concerning Marxist art literature in the Asian and Latin American countries, which is very different from the European point of view, an entire manual could be written. Only a few books of this kind are available in European libraries. The works by Alice Guillermo[69] show typical traits of Marxism in developing countries. After having actively supported a revolutionary movement in her native country in the 1970s, she published several studies about the social tendency in Philippine painting. In her writings, she emphasized the thesis that the culture of the developing countries is still completely dependent on patterns of the Western industrialized countries.[70] This very convincing thesis seems to have disappeared from the theoretical debate after 1990. Nonetheless, certain countries have further developed and renewed these reflections, in particular on the basis of the association of social and political thought that comes from native traditions and from certain Marxist theories.

[68] John Roberts, ed., *Art Has No History! The Making and Unmaking of Modern Art* (London: Verso, 1994).

[69] Alice Guillermo, *Social Realism in the Philippines* (Manila: Asphodel, 1987); Alice Guillermo, "The Institutions of the Modern Art World in the Philippines," in *Modernity in Asian Art*, ed. John Clark, The University of Sydney East Asian Series 7 (Broadway, Australia: Wild Peony, 1993), 116–27; Alice Guillermo, *Protest/Revolutionary Art in the Philippines 1970–1990* (Quezon City: University of the Philippines Press, 2001).

[70] Guillermo, *The Institutions*, 126.

3. CONTEXT

●

The evolution of Marxist philosophy is influenced by other directions of reasoning. Thus, the historical development and present state of Marxist sciences cannot be understood without discussing their non-Marxist counterparts, in particular sociology of art and anarchist thought. There is a danger that the whole body of Marxist art literature will no longer be part of the general consciousness in the near future. The few works that belong to the accepted canon are sometimes already relabeled as "sociology of art."

3.1. BOURGEOIS ART HISTORY

○

Modern schools of bourgeois art history have their roots in the second half of the nineteenth century when art history was institutionalized at the universities. Little has changed since then. The conception of bourgeois art history can be understood as a stable and continuous flow that has remained dominant until the present day. Still, after such a long time, it shows signs of becoming a fossilized form. One characteristic is its clinging to certain dogmas that have already been rejected as wrong or outdated by other branches of social sciences. Other signs of its decline are its revolving on its own axis without moving forward and its actual hagiography regarding its own history.

Art history as the history of style

Art history as the history of styles is one of the oldest methods of art history, which still constitutes a basic method of this discipline. "Style" has always been defined not only as categorization of the visible forms on the surface of works of art, but also by more abstract components such as the development of technology at a certain stage of history and a multitude of other factors. For someone who is not well-acquainted with this matter, it might be surprising that "style" was and still is a central category of Marxist art history. One of the reasons for this is that Marxist art history came into being during a time in which the history of styles was still the dominant method in art history. There are various components that are the same in bourgeois and Marxist art history. For instance, Heinrich Wölfflin speaks of style as a non-individual expression of a certain epoch. It is not the result of the genius of an individual artist, but an output of the *Formwollen*[1] – in other words, the common predilection of all members of a society for certain artistic forms. However, the parallels with Marxist conceptions end here, since Wölfflin stresses the idea of the "style of the school, the country and the race."[2] In contrast to this kind of thought, in Marxist art history the style is regarded as an impersonal manifestation of a certain mode of production molding all objects that are called "art" of a certain epoch. This definition of style embraces a multitude of other factors, but these differ considerably from those that are considered in traditional definitions of style. The categorization systems of the nineteenth century were certainly preparing the basis for later Marxist ordering systems of style, but the latter has subordinated the concept of "style" to its specific model of history and its class theory. Such a conception broke radically with traditional art history. The haute bourgeois ideology which penetrates all writings by Wölfflin is diametrically opposed to Marxist thought, even when his vision of "art history without the artist"contains the idea of a "collective will."[3] Yet, this "collective will" has been defined by German art historians in the late nineteenth and early twentieth-centuries as the will of the "race," and, by taking the later results of this kind of nationalist ideology into consideration, we have to recognize that art history of Wölfflin's generation had generally been the antipode of Marxist art history.

Origins of Marxist art history

An analysis of the argumentation and methods of Marxist art history reveals that it is not the German or English, but rather the liberal French tradition that had a certain impact. The most prominent supporters of this direction were involved in the so-called *bataille réaliste* of the 1840s and 1850s. During this period, literati such as Théophile Thoré, Edmond Duranty, and Champfleury fought against the bourgeois establishment. Judgment of certain painters and works of art and their respective classification in certain social classes had already been made by these authors. Their views, however, have nothing in common with the later sociology, but were based on ideas on the social order, which had their origin in utopian

[1] The expression *Formwollen* created by Wölfflin bears a certain mystical sense that denotes the abstract desire of all individuals of a certain society to create a certain "form" in art and architecture.

[2] Heinrich Wölfflin, *Kunstgeschichtliche Grundbegriffe. Das Problem der Stilentwicklung in der neueren Kunst* (Munich: Bruckmann, 1915; 8th ed. cited here, Dresden: Verlag der Kunst, 1984), 14.

[3] On the discussion concerning Wölfflin, see Hadjinicolaou, *Class Struggle*, 59–62.

socialism. "Style" played a huge role in the writings of French left-liberal authors. Discussion focused on the styles of realism and naturalism, which were interpreted as the manifestation of a social consciousness amongst the artists. In the course of the second half of the nineteenth century, modern thought, free of nationalist or racist ideas elaborated in France. Certain styles are already assigned to different social classes, although these classes are not defined in a sociological sense. For instance, these authors clearly identify the "bourgeoisie" as a supporting and producing class regarding the high culture of their time. Another source of left-liberal literature of the nineteenth century is, of course, French sociology of art, which initially became known through the writings of Hippolyte Taine (see chapter 3.3).

From the October Revolution onwards, the main source of Marxist art history was historical materialism and class theory. The idea that style is the material visualization of the ideology of certain classes is the result of a profound study of Marx's philosophy in the early Soviet Union. From this came the hypotheses the artists themselves expressed in different styles, like a chameleon changes its colors, to win the approval of the economic and political leading classes. The heterogeneity of style within the œuvre of an individual artist is often ignored in bourgeois art history. Accordingly, if traditional history of style and Marxist art history are compared, there are few reference points. The uniform outward appearance of certain works of art—in short, the style—is not the result of an unconscious common will, race, temper, artistic genius, etc. Rather, the uniform outward appearance of works of artcomes from art techniques, ways of production, and from the function of high art to visualize the ideology of the leading class. The outward appearance of a work of art reveals much more of the ideology of the patrons than of the artist.

Iconography

Iconography is a method to decode the former sense of a work of art with the help of certain "signs" included in a picture, sculpture, etc. Since it is a technique to decipher the hidden sense of a work of art, it operates on another level than Marxist art history, which is part of a world view and not a specialized research technique. From the beginnings of artistic creation, pictures and sculptures were equipped with signs and symbols that contained a certain magical, religious, or social meaning. During the period of their production, a greater number of people were able to decipher these icons. In later periods, the correct interpretation of these signs vanished or it became the exclusive skill of a chosen group, for instance priests.

A short definition of iconography is as follows: the initial message of a painting or a sculpture is expounded with the help of all pictorial and written historical aids, such as reference works on the meaning of certain religious signs. Iconography is a neutral instrument of analysis. However, most of the publications written on iconography are molded by bourgeois interest, but there is also a very small stock of art historical literature in which iconography is interpreted according to Marxist philosophy (see chapter

2.3, Schapiro, and chapter 2.4, Zschelletzschky). The iconographical interpretation of a picture with certain symbols and figures by two different art historians whose ideologies are opposed to each other can lead to similar results—given the case that there are historically unambiguous and definite sources of iconographical decoding, such as picture books with explanations of certain pictorial signs. However, the neutrality of iconography seems to be nothing like pure theory: in reality, in nearly all cases bourgeois and Marxist iconographical analysis stand in total contradiction to each other.

Iconology

Whereas iconography is focused on the visual language of certain objects and is restricted to the interpretation of these objects, the concept of *iconology* is much wider. Here, the message of a work of art is not only examined through the hidden meaning of its signs, but its historical background, explanation of the intentions of patrons, the social class of patrons and the recipients, and the reasons for choice of certain themes could be part of the research framework. Furthermore, several other points are significant. For instance, research may focus on why a specific work of art had been commissioned for a certain locality, who exactly the commissioners were, and for which public the work was planned. In short, iconology embraces a much wider field than iconography. The subjects of investigation are not fixed in a commonly accepted canon. Because the class of patrons and the class of recipients play a certain role, iconology shows a similarity to social history of art. Nevertheless, the latter can be easily distinguished from the first: social history of art is indispensable connected with political commentary concerning a certain time and economic system or ajudgment on certain sovereigns, ruling dynasties, or the ruling social class, whereas in iconology an open political comment concerning a certain historical event is strictly avoided. Another difference is the interpretation of the pictorial signs themselves: in iconology, the interpretation refers strictly to the historical sources and does not go beyond them; in social history of art, however, the interpretation is freer and more focused, towards the contemporary sociological or political understanding of these signs. The economic and historical evolution assumes a central position in social history of art, but this is not the case in iconology, where matters of economy are debated at length but only in order to interpret a specific group of works of art and its aim is not to enlighten the political context of the whole epoch. Iconology fails to integrate political aspects into the analysis and integrate the political dimension of a certain epoch.

Written by Aby Warburg, *Bildniskunst und florentinisches Bürgertum* (1902)[4] is an early contribution to this method. During the period of its creation, his deliberations on the Florentine portrait of the Renaissance

[4] Aby Warburg, *Bildniskunst und florentinisches Bürgertum* (Leipzig: Seemann, 1902).

expanded historical studies into different new fields. For instance, the book contains a psychological description of central figures from the Florentine ruling class. Presented with subtle irony and a certain sense of humor, the style of Warburg freed itself from the conventions of his time. Today, both the man and his work are overrated in an almost absurd manner. Iconology marked a trend that had already been visible in French and English art history in 1900. It had been a logical consequence of the endeavors to connect an analysis of specific icons with the class of commissioners and recipients. In this respect, *Florentine Painting* (1948) by Antal contains some traits of this method. But these similarities are only of a superficial nature: iconology shows no relationship to the Marxist model of history.

There can be no doubt that the elitist ideology of the Warburg school prevented the further development of iconology in the direction of a socially engaged art history. In later writings, the field of analysis became restricted, such as in *Painting and Experience in 15th Century Italy* (1972)[5] by M. Baxandall. The question must be posed as to whether the heirs of Warburg really stand in line with his progressive conception of art history, or whether the Warburg Institute became a symbol of conservative European art history. The sad decline of the journal of the same name seems to support this hypothesis.

cultural studies

Cultural studies, formerly named *history of civilizations*, do not belong to art history. From the late twentieth century on, the term "cultural studies" was expanded to denote all sorts of scientific research in the fields of human creative activities. In these studies a multitude of different factors are matters of research: development of culture in general, economy and technology, religious notions and other metaphysical conceptions, furthermore, folkloristic, philosophical, sociological, psychological aspects could be part of the research. The number of research subjects and their combinations is practically limitless. The border between cultural studies and other branches of science is diffuse and often not well defined. A classical work is *Art and Society* (1937)[6] by Herbert Read. At the time of its publication, Antal saw a certain relationship to his own method. The multitude of different themes in Read's publications led some people to believe that his standpoint was politically progressive. However, even in *Art and Society*, the different factors upon which the analysis of various world civilizations of the past and present is based is very vaguely defined. The sociological analysis is superficial, and the picture of history created by the author shows no relation to historical materialism. The book has the character of an essay, which is interesting. Nevertheless, from the late 1960s on, when the number of cultural studies was in full expansion, the texts related to this discipline

[5] Michael Baxandall, *Painting and Experience in Fifteenth Century Italy: A Primer in the Social History of Pictorial Style* (Oxford: Oxford University Press, 1972).

[6] Herbert Edward Read, *Art and Society* (London: William Heinemann, 1937).

were often interpreted to be modern and forward-looking, since they exposed an interest in popular art, contemporary art and other uncommon themes. The term "cultural study" per se is a neutral one. Today, it refers to a new scientific discipline and not to a specific method: open to all ideological directions, it is not linked specifically to progressive or left-wing thought.

3.2. SOCIAL HISTORY OF ART

It is interesting to compare social history of art with Marxist art history, since it occupies the transitional field between left-wing thought and historical materialism. Considering that the Marxist standpoint in art history and theory was not a possible position in most countries of the world, the creation of social history was the logical consequence. It has integrated elements of economic thought, sometimes even of sociological theory, but always of materialist philosophies. In Great Britain, social history of art embraces a relatively wide field of observation, and its position within universities seems much better than in other European countries where it seems to play a minor important role. Social history of art is based on a generally accepted number of points:

- Social history of art is interested in the relations between economy, technology (especially of art techniques) and political history in connection with the development of art. The history of economics plays a central role. There is the consciousness that certain phases of economy and technology development produce specific forms of art.
- Social history of art is not necessarily bound to a thorough knowledge of Marxism, but among many other things, certain theories of it are discussed. Some principal theories of Marxism, such as class theory, are strictly avoided. The basis of social history is a materialist philosophy, often identical to a bourgeois-liberal view of the world.
- It is an important fact that a description of political history connected with art history does not produce a social history, because this method is based on a multitude of perspectives, of which political history is only one of many.

Social history is not necessarily fixed on a certain political standpoint. In some cases it defends right-wing or even nationalistic views. Because of this, we can differentiate between non-Marxist and Marxist conceptions of social history (see chapter 4.2). The origins of this method are certainly in the historiography of the universities, even when a slight influence of French sociology of art of the nineteenth century can be detected (see chapter 3.3). The aim of social history of art is to expound the economic and social framework in which the evolution of art takes place.

Origins in British historiography

It originates in the endeavors of British historians of the 1940s to create a new direction of history writing.[7] In art history, some of Aby Warburg's writings show traces of the new method. A fully developed social history of art was first presented with such works as Antal's *Florentine Painting* (1948), which contains an overview of the economic, sociological, religious, and political background of the historical period in question in the introductory chapter. Another important work is *Art and the Industrial Revolution* (1947) by Francis D. Klingender. However, since Antal and Klingender both exhibit a pronounced class-related standpoint, they have to be ordered into the direction of Marxist history (see chapter 2.2), which can be understood as an early developmental stage of social history. As a logical consequence of political history of the 1950s marked by the destructive force of the Cold War, the Marxist influence was replaced by a sort of diluted historiography.

A representative work of the following period is *Picasso* (1965)[8] by John Berger. Although the author expounds the historical, economic, and sociological background, his idea of a direct influence of these factors on Picasso's paintings seems simplistic. This genre of social history avoids a deeper class analysis, and even the economic basis of art is treated only in passing. Such works are grounded in the idea that high art is based on a closed system of thought that is only loosely related to the general evolution of the economy or to contemporary society.

The impulse of 1968

During the 1960s, a great number of young scholars contributed to the emergence of a new social history in the Anglophone countries. But even in these progressive times, *History of the Comic Strip* (1973/1990)[9] by David Kunzle was an outstanding example. The volume of 1973 contains single-sheet prints and printed graphic series from 1450 until 1825, which are normally not considered to belong to the history of the comic strip. With his work David Kunzle has completely renewed the view of a traditional genre of art. Many attempts to redefine the principles and methods of art history mark the period between 1968 and 1979.

In Germany, there had been an attempt by Jutta Held and Norbert Schneider to establish a school of social history. Both were influenced by the Critical Theory.[10] At the end of the twentieth century, the publications by Jutta Held were debated and well known among art historians. She was probably one of the great independent personalities of German art history.[11]

---

7 Frederick Antal, "Remarks on the Method of Art History," in *Burlington Magazine* 91 (1949): 49–50.

8 John Berger, *The Success and Failure of Picasso* (Harmondsworth: Penguin Books, 1965).

9 David Kunzle, *History of the Comic Strip*, vol. 1, *The Early Comic Strip: Narrative Strips and Picture Stories in the European Broadsheet from c. 1450 to 1825* (Berkeley: University of California Press, 1973; Kunzle, *History of the Comic Strip*, vol. 2, *The Nineteenth Century* (Berkeley: University of California Press, 1990).

10 Jutta Held and Norbert Schneider, *Sozialgeschichte der Malerei vom Spätmittelalter bis ins 20. Jahrhundert* (Cologne: DuMont, 1993).

11 Jutta Held and Guernica-Gesellschaft, eds., *Der spanische Bürgerkrieg und die bildenden Künste*, Schriften der Guernica-Gesellschaft 1 (Hamburg: Argument, 1989); Martin Papenbrock, Gisela Schirmer, eds., *Kunst und Sozialgeschichte* (Pfaffenweiler: Centaurus, 1995).

A new stage of social history was initiated by Timothy J. Clark, who is regarded as the most important Marxist art historian of the late twentieth century in the literature of the English-speaking countries.[12] However, one must question the real Marxist nature of his Marxism. His two most important books are *The Image of the People: Gustave Courbet and the 1848 Revolution* (1973)[13] and *The Absolute Bourgeois* (1973).[14] Here, the author analyzes culture, politics, and economic history in France in the periods immediately before and after the revolution of 1848. The introduction to *Image of the People*, entitled "On the Social History of Art," has the character of a manifesto. Clark distances himself from all hitherto accepted instruments of social history: he rejects the analysis of ideologies of classes, the social structure and even political history, thus he also refuses the idea that artistic creation is linked to society. Consequently, the "new art history" of Clark rejects all epistemological instruments of former Marxist research of the 1940s and 1950s. Both the literary structure of his manifesto and its general argumentation undoubtedly come from modern art theory of the 1960s. They have nothing to do with Marxism and absolutely nothing in common with the different directions of socialist thought.

Image of the People contains certain issues that oppose the method of social history and others that agree with it. Social engagement of the artist is observed with great interest, but it is more the view of the naturalist observing a rare insect under a magnifying glass. The idea that art can support social change is rejected—which might be, of course, a realistic standpoint—but this also can be interpreted as a certain degree of sarcasm concerning social commitment of the artist. Accordingly, he reduces the revolution of 1848 to a bacchanalian festivity that was doomed to fail. In his eyes, history shows no concrete movement towards a certain direction; only the "I" is the driving force behind all human activities. All these points support the assumption that Clark had been influenced by a kind of anarchist thought that became popular in Western Europe and North America in the late 1960s.

In the second decade of the twenty-first century, judgement of the New Left has become conflicting; it was a positive attempt to propagate anti-authoritarian thought and this brought a moment of liberation into the bourgeois society, but the New Left was a heterogeneous movement, which tended in very different political directions. Nevertheless, it brought a breath of fresh air to a rigid and immobile society.

---

[12] Harris, *New Art History*, 63–93; Hemingway, *Marxism and the History of Art*, 191; Carter, *Renew Marxist Art History*, 50.

[13] Timothy J. Clark, *The Image of the People: Gustave Courbet and the 1848 Revolution* (London: Thames & Hudson, 1973).

[14] Timothy J. Clark, *The Absolute Bourgeois: Artists and Politics in France 1848–1851* (London: Thames & Hudson, 1973).

3.3. SOCIOLOGY OF ART

In the course of the twentieth century, Marxist theories on art had often been assigned to sociology of art, and this has caused a certain confusion. Sometimes close to the vocabulary of Marxism and that of other socialist directions, the terminology of sociology itself has caused this uncertainty. This is the reason why the general public, but also students and historians of art erroneously associate sociology with left-wing thought.

Sociology systematically describes the social structure of society and the laws of its evolution. It is a basic discipline of social sciences whose development has followed a very different track to those of art history. Since sociology is concerned with interactions between social groups and investigates the functions of all kinds of communicative structures, the cultural and artistic activities constitute one of its fields of research. From the middle of the nineteenth century on, there had been various attempts to connect sociology, which was a newly established discipline at this time, with aesthetics. These disparate efforts formed a unity with a very heterogeneous character, and the discipline of sociology of art remained poorly well defined, even today. A brief definition of it will constitute the theoretical basis of the following subchapters:

- Sociology of art is not concerned with the description of works of art nor deliberations on its aesthetical values and is not an account of the historical background of works of art.
- It aims to describe the social process related to the creation, distribution, and reception of art and culture in general. The social position of the artists, of the patrons and of the recipients of art is another important theme of sociology.
- There are two basically different methods: French "sociological aesthetics," which was created after 1850, and "empirical art sociology," which originates in American sociology of the 1930s.

Sociological aesthetics

Created in France, the term *esthétique sociologique*[15] ("sociological aesthetics") precisely refers to what is designated by long periphrases in German such as "*Soziologie der Darstellungssysteme*" ("sociology of depiction systems") and "*Soziologie als ästhetische Wahrnehmung*" ("sociology as aesthetical perception"). Professors of aesthetics, of literary criticism, of philosophy, of music theory, sometimes of art history, of sociology, and academics from other branches of social sciences have written the first texts.

[15] This expression was coined by Charles Lalo in his book *L'art et la vie sociale* (Paris: Doin, 1921).

The philosophy of aesthetics is the basis of sociological aesthetics, whereas empirical art sociology was exclusively a matter of research by sociologists. If the discipline of sociology of art is analyzed in its entire historical evolution, it becomes obvious that the influence of Marxism on it had always been marginal.

French sociology of art of the nineteenth century

French sociological aesthetics is the starting point for all later variants of sociology of art. It is present in a mature form in *Philosophie de l'Art* (1865–1869/1882)[16] by Hippolyte Taine. It displays all the characteristic features of this direction that are still valid today. Typically, the influence of classes on the evolution of art plays a marginal role in the general structure of this work. Taine analyzes the whole œuvre of an artist which he assigns to a school or a style. But he broke with the conception of the "school of painting", promoted by art history of his time, since he intended to analyze this "school" in an ensemble much vaster: the *milieu* or civilization. The school objectivizes and transfers certain leanings, values, and ideas of contemporary society into artistic forms. To expound the connections of a school with society, Taine refers to notions such as "race," "epoch," "historical moment," "developing stage of art techniques" and "philosophical ideas". His book is not based on empirical research—this method was still not known in the 1860s—but on art history, whose methods it renewed. This sociological sub-discipline is founded first of all in reflections on aesthetics, but it also takes into consideration the influence of the technological evolution (particularly those of depiction techniques) as well as the influence of society on the evolution of arts. Even the creation of new aesthetical forms is analyzed through this lens. Sociological aesthetics intends to identify the structures or the "laws" according to which the evolution of arts is taking place. Taking its sources from materialist philosophies, French sociological aesthetics has influenced social history of art of the twentieth century (see chapter 3.2).

Another important book of sociology of art *Du principe de l'art et sa destination sociale* (1865) by Pierre-Joseph Proudhon (see chapter 2.1), is not a sociological work in a strict sense since it mixes different things together, for instance, utopian socialist art theory and deliberations on the evolution of art. We can also call it the first mature book on socialist art theory. *Du principe de l'art* is like a strangely shimmering diamond that shows various and different things that are not normally grouped together in unity. One of the surprising aspects of this book is that the author already connects a certain style to a specific developing stage of society. *Du principe de l'art* remains a central text regarding sociology of art as well as socialist art

[16] Hippolyte Taine, *Philosophie de l'Art* (Paris: G. Baillière et Cie 1865–1869; 2nd rev. ed., Paris: G. Baillière et Cie, 1882).

literature. Proudhon's ideas on art found further development in *L'art au point de vue sociologique* (1889)[17] by Jean-Marie Guyau. This book seems to have been widely disseminated all over Europe, since it presented some of Proudhon's thoughts on a social art in agreement with the common sense of the Third Republic.

Sociology of art in 1900

In the period between 1900 and 1933, sociology of art in Belgium and Germany stood under the influence of Marxism and other directions of socialist thought. One formative example is the essay *Soziologische Aesthetik* (1896)[18] by Georg Simmel, who was near to the standpoint of German social democracy in these years. Another example is the book *Essais socialistes* (1906)[19] by Emile Vandervelde. In the third chapter of this booklet, entitled *L'art*, the economic situation of the artist under capitalism is analyzed from different aspects. The basics of Vandervelde's research are not empirical studies in today's sense, but rather an observation of reality, especially concerning the social status and salaries of artists in relation to their class origins. Vandervelde makes some deliberations on artistic freedom in a future socialist society. The chapter *L'art* of the *Essais socialistes* seems to be a classical work of sociology of art that is based on profound deliberations. The booklet is not very well known today.

During the years between 1900 and 1914, theorizing on art and society came into fashion among bourgeois intellectuals. Examples are articles and books written by Wilhelm Hausenstein. However, the progressive period marks only a very short intermezzo in Hausenstein's work, whose opinions turned in the conservative direction in the 1950s. It is surprising that he had intended to create a Marxist history of art in the 1910s. An example is the article *Versuch einer Soziologie der bildenden Künste* (1913)[20] in which he tries to connect the "material" of the works of art with certain elements of the stage model of historical materialism. The source of this kind of thought might be publications by Engels from the 1880s. The essay by Hausenstein shows no relationship with Soviet Marxist art history of the 1920s. However, reflecting on the material dimension of works on art marks a preliminary stage of Marxist art history and archaeology.

Marxist art sociology

The most important Marxist sociologist of the Weimar Republic was Lu Märten.[21] She wrote a book on the economic situation of female artists entitled *Die Künstlerin* (1914)[22] and two others on questions related to

---

17 Jean-Marie Guyau, *L'art au point de vue sociologique* (Paris: F. Alcan, 1889).

18 Georg Simmel, "Soziologische Aesthetik," *Die Zukunft* 17 (1896): 204–16.

19 Emile Vandervelde, *Essais socialistes. L'alcoolisme – la religion – l'art* (Paris: F. Alcan, 1906).

20 Wilhelm Hausenstein, "Versuch einer Soziologie der bildenden Kunst," *Archiv für Sozialwissenschaft und Sozialpolitik* 36 (1913): 758–94.

21 She used different pseudonyms to sign her satirical and political essays. The full name reads Luisa Charlotte Märten.

22 Lu Märten, *Die Künstlerin* (Munich: Langen, 1914).

social art entitled *Historisch-Materialistisches* (1921)[23] and *Wesen und Veränderungen der Formen und Künste* (1924).[24] In her books, Märten attributes different forms of art (music, literature, fine arts, applied arts) to different classes of society, and another topic she contemplates is the social status of artists. Her ideas show a strong similarity to writings of the Soviet minister of culture Anatoly Lunacharsky and mirror the debates on a new art that took place in the early Soviet Union. Especially her brochure *Historisch-Materialistisches* is reminiscent of Soviet writings about the question of a new workers' culture. Without a doubt, Lu Märten was the founder of a Marxist sociology of art in Germany.

Critical Theory of the Frankfurt school

Shortly before 1933 at the Frankfurt Institute of Social Research, new endeavors emerged to enlarge the field of sociology to all aspects of culture and mass communication. The most prominent example and a key text on sociology is *The Work of Art in the Age of its Mechanical Reproduction* (1936)[25] by Walter Benjamin. After the Second World War, the theory of the Frankfurt school became a new starting point of sociology in Germany. Written by Theodor Adorno and Max Horkheimer *Dialectic of Enlightenment* (1947)[26] contains a chapter on the culture industry of the twentieth century. The Frankfurt school dominated the progressive debates in Germany from the late 1960s until the 1980s. After 1990, it seems that critical theory continued to exist.[27]

French sociology of art of the twentieth century

Up until the early twentieth century, French sociology of art was one of the most progressive forms of philosophizing on the arts. But afterwards it showed signs of a certain decline. A typical representative of this last period was Pierre Francastel. His work received a certain degree of interest in the 1960s. But Francastel was a representative of theorizing on aesthetics; an analysis of social stratification and its relation to art was not part of his sociology. Many of his texts subtly aimed to show the superiority of French culture. He presented an idiosyncratic mixture of different thoughts; for example, his essay *Destruction d'un espace plastique* (1952)[28] contains various meditations on the development of perspective since the Renais-

[23] Lu Märten, *Historisch-Materialistisches über Wesen und Veränderung der Künste* [Historical-materialistic thought on the nature and change of the arts] (Berlin: Junge Garde, 1921). The first expression in the German title is a play on words.

[24] Lu Märten, *Wesen und Veränderung der Formen und Künste. Resultate historisch-materialistischer Untersuchungen* [Nature and changes in forms and arts: Results of historical materialistic research] (Berlin: Taifun Verlag, 1924).

[25] Walter Benjamin, "L'œuvre d'art à l'époque de sa reproduction mécanisée," *Zeitschrift für Sozialforschung* 5 (1936): 40–66.

[26] Max Horkheimer and Theodor Adorno, *Dialektik der Aufklärung* (Amsterdam: Querido, 1947).

[27] Marcus Hawel and Moritz Blanke, eds., *Kritische Theorie der Krise* (Berlin: Dietz, 2012).

[28] Pierre Francastel, "Destruction d'un espace plastique" (1952), in *Études de sociologie de l'art* (Paris: Denoël Gonthier, 1970), 191–252.

sance, and its general argumentation is that modern non-perspective systems (invented by French painters) are superior to mathematically based systems. Francastel was influenced by contemporary French art theory and to a lesser degree by sociological or art historical facts.

Empirical sociology of art

The second main stream of sociology of art, which represents *empirical sociology of art*, originated in US-American research methods from the first half of the twentieth century. In that country, sociology was a firm element of the academic curriculum at the universities, which might explain the superior position of US sociology from the 1930s until the 1950s. Since empirical research on different target groups play a huge role in the American economy, it was a logical step to transfer this method to other subjects of research, like art. American Sociology in this period was mainly centered on social functions in society, but some sociologists were also interested in Weberian analysis. Profiting from a stable and liberal background, US sociology occupied a globally dominant position for several decades. Since its instruments of analysis need hefty financial support, empirical sociology, despite its claim of neutrality, is nonetheless subservient to the interests of certain dominant groups. But if the data basis and framework of research are well considered beforehand, empirical sociology can show interesting results.

Introduction to the Sociology of Art (1940)[29] by Adolph S. Tomars constitutes the first mature work on empirical sociology of art. Even if it does not contain empirical research, in contrast to latter publications according to this method, it is based on a modern sociology that means the function model developed by Robert MacIver. This sociologist held the idea that in history, the class structure changed several times from a corporate class system (estate society) to a competitive class system (changing multiplicity of classes in a competitive economy).[30] Tomars uses the example of classical Greek art to show that the idealizing character of sculpture served to glorify the upper class, whereas for the lower classes, naturalistic or satirical modes of depiction were chosen. This hierarchy of depiction modes corresponds to the corporative class system. Later, in Hellenism, a change to more dynamic economics took place that caused a certain kind of social mobility between the classes. In this new competitive class system, modes of depiction caused a change of the poles of "idealistic" and "realistic." At the end of his book, Tomars applied this model to his own time, the late 1930s: he interpreted American abstract painting as a sign of the competitive social system of the USA with its dynamic economics and its patchwork of quickly changing class cleavages, and therefore it is interpreted as a symbol

---

[29] Adolph S. Tomars, *Introduction to the Sociology of Art* (Mexico City: n.p., 1940).

[30] In an abbreviated form explained in Robert Morrison MacIver, *Society: A Textbook of Sociology* (London: Macmillian, 1937), 174–75.

of a positive period of history. Adopting some axioms of former European left-wing art theory, Tomar's book seems to be very progressive at first glance, but its general tendency is something completely opposite. In the 1970s, when sociology of art became very fashionable and received some attention from the general public, the quality of some publications became dubious. There were an enormous number of empirical studies regarding the social position of artists and those of visitors of museums,—but these presented results that had no relationship with reality. For instance, in a German empirical study, one could read that the income of German painters was very high, that they all enjoyed a good reputation, and that they were all very satisfied with teaching of the academies of fine arts[31].

The best-known work of empirical sociology of art is *La distinction* (1979)[32] by Pierre Bourdieu. The extent to which this work contains Marxist axioms is still a matter of debate today. Its general structure is surely Weberian. It exposes a new system of categorization based on the old idea of status groups as communities of human beings who share the same social behavior, lifestyle, etc. Bourdieu included a multiplicity of stratification variables in his research on the cultural behavior of the different classes of contemporary society.

Books that deal with sociology from an art historical perspective

Today, sociology of art in the Western countries is marked by an ideology that is opposed to critical thought and could be radically distinguished from Marxism. However, after 1960 a new direction appeared that shows an interesting relationship with the critical direction in social sciences and establishes a link between sociological empirical research and history of art. An example of this is *Canvases and Careers* (1965)[33] by the art historian Cynthia A. White and the sociologist Harrison C. White. The book is largely unknown in the majority of European countries, but its theme is of central importance. It demonstrates that the origins of modern art, especially of impressionism, had been preceded by changes in institutions and the art market. With the help of statistical data (number of exhibitions, prices of pictures, sales, etc.) it shows that the dominant position of state institutions in the field of fine arts had been subordinated due to the priority of the private market. The social position of patrons and artists is not a core issue of this research, but rather the focus of the research is on the changes in institutions. The thought behind this direction of American art sociology is

---

31 Andreas Johannes Wiesand, "20 Fragen zum Berufsfeld Bildende Kunst," in *Kunstsoziologie. Bildende Kunst und Gesellschaft*, ed. Rainer Wick and Astrid Wick-Kmoch (Cologne: DuMont, 1979), 157–90.

32 Pierre Bourdieu, *La distinction. Critique sociale du judgement* (Paris: Éd. de Minuit, 1979). Translated by Richard Nice as *Distinction: A Social Critique on the Judgement of Taste* (London: Routledge & Kegan Paul, 1984).

33 Harrison C. White and Cynthia A. White, *Canvases and Careers: Institutional Change in the French Painting World* (New York: John Wiley & Sons, 1965). The reprint of 1993 contains a new chapter on American art sociology of the 1960s and a bibliographical list of similar works.

far from the former critical direction in art history, but to some degree it displays similar features.

After 1990, some investigations which associate empirical sociology with art history were published in Europe. In Germany, a history of documentary photography entitled *Klassenbilder* (2007/2010)[34] by the sociologist Rudolf Stumberger has found a larger audience. Some art historians have used sociology as an instrument of recognition, for instance Norbert Schneider and Oliver Sukrow. The exhibition catalog *Abschied von Ikarus* (2012)[35], which took a new view of the painting of the former German Democratic Republic, received a controversial reception from the German public. The title of the catalog, *Farewell from Icarus*, refers to the dreams of German communists to create art for the common people, a dream that died in 1990.

In the twentieth-first century, sociological works have more or less replaced the former history of art influenced by Marxism or marked by social history of art. But today's sociology of art is incapable of filling the many loopholes in documentation regarding art history: thus, many themes fall through the cracks of research or have remained unexplored. Contemporary research encounters the same problems as history of art. It is under heavy economic pressure; its methodology and borderlines to other disciplines of social sciences become less well defined.

3.4. ANARCHISM AND ART LITERATURE

This chapter aims to give a short introduction to a theme that would need a much deeper explanation. Belonging to the sphere of political philosophy, anarchism has nearly no relationship to the history of art. In Anglo-American literature, it is often confused with Marxist philosophy since it shares with it an antibourgeois and anticapitalist view combined with a revolutionary attitude.

There are many reasons why anarchist thought in contemporary culture and social sciences has scarcely been analyzed: its negative denotation, its political history, and the difficulties in finding a commonly accepted definition. Two things are certain: first, there are many different directions of anarchist thought, and secondly, there are surprising similarities to Marxism.

---

[34] Rudolf Stumberger, *Klassen-Bilder. Sozialdokumentarische Fotografie 1900–1945* (Constance: UVK, 2007); Stumberger, *Klassenbilder II. Sozialdokumentarische Fotografie 1950–2000* (Constance: UVK, 2010).

[35] Karl-Siegbert Rehberg, ed., *Abschied von Ikarus. Bildwelten der DDR – neu gesehen*, exhib. cat., Neues Museum Weimar, 19 Oct. 2012 – 3 Feb. 2013 (Cologne: König, 2012).

Even Marx in his early writings propagated ideas that he himself later regarded as anarchist, such as the disappearance of the family and the state in a socialist society. In addition, in certain works of the late Engels, for instance his *Origin of the Family* (1884), we find long passages that, if we did not know the real author, seem to be written by an anarchist thinker. On the other hand, the difference to main directions of anarchism had already been expounded at length in the *German Ideology*, in the polemic against Max Stirner, and in the pamphlets by Marx against Proudhon, Bakunin etc. As a result, the borderline between the two ideologies had already been well defined in the mid nineteenth century. The following short definition aims to help separate the two opposite directions:[36]

- The nucleus of anarchist thought is the idea of the disappearance of the state in a society based on principles of human solidarity. Future society should be organized in small collectives. However, some directions of anarchism are not occupied with such notions at all, because, here, individual freedom and the dominance of the "I" play the main role.
- Anarchist thought is a materialist and antiauthoritarian philosophy, rejecting bourgeois morals and social behavior, as well as common social norms and laws.
- The writings of Max Stirner, Pierre-Joseph Proudhon, Michail Bakunin, and Petr Kropotkin are the bases of different directions of anarchism (individual anarchism, socio-revolutionary anarchism and forms of anarcho-syndicalism).

Synonyms of the term "anarchism"

If anarchism is nearly completely absent as a category in art theory, it was, perhaps, because in the past different left-wing movements were qualified in a negative sense as "anarchism", but without really presenting a convincing definition of it. Up until the Spanish Civil War, anarchism had been understood as a variant of socialist thought and was used as synonym for "libertarian socialism," "left-wing radicalism," "radical theory", etc.[37] In modern literature, the word is either consciously or subconsciously avoided. However, anarchism is not the negative opposite to Marxism, since certain principal theories of anarchist thought are the same in radical variants of Marxism.

Differences to Marxism

The difference between anarchism and Marxism will be expounded in the following sections. The major point of difference is that the various directions of anarchism pay little attention to the theory of political economy and instead focus on other factors, such as biological nature, "nature" as such, ideas, psychological factors, philosophy, etc. In writings by anarchist

[36] This definition is based on the following sources: Tom Bottomore, Laurence Harris, V. G. Kiernan, and Ralph Miliband, eds., *A Dictionary of Marxist Thought* (Cambridge, MA: Harvard University Press, 1983), 18–19.

[37] Alex Prichard, Ruth Kinna, Saku Pinta, and David Berry, eds., *Libertarian Socialism: Politics in Black and Red* (Basingstoke: Palgrave Macmillan, 2012).

authors, economics is an exotic and mysterious thing that produces goods and commercial services. Since anarchism reacts against the state and authoritarian thought, it heavily agitates against capitalism as a supporting system. In contrast to this, Marxism declares the state as the primary player in guiding the economy and society and, furthermore, analyzes all social actions of the human as being guided by the economic background. Some variants of anarchism are indifferent regarding the question of the state and a political change, and propagate instead the idea that a change of society depends first of all on an individual transformation of the human mind.

Vision of history of anarchism

The models of history of the various directions of anarchism all differ considerably from Marxist historical materialism. In *Mutual Aid* (1902)[38] by Petr Kropotkin, we find a model of history that displays a typical thinking pattern also found in many later writings by anarchist authors. This model is more wavelike; it changes from a positive to a negative pole and back. Corresponding with the positive pole, the first stage is primitive early societies that are described as an association of free individuals. The second stage refers to early advanced civilizations of antiquity, which is already marked by an inversion of the curve, since the majority of human beings was violently oppressed by forms of authoritarian power. It was not before the Middle Ages that a return to a positive state was reached. Peasants were organized in autonomous village societies and craftsmen in guilds. The state was weak and had little influence on these communities with their self-organizing and independent economies. The Middle Ages represent a developed stage of civilization without reprisals of the state. The decline began with the centralized state of modern times in which the individual is oppressed: solidarity among human beings and freedom are destroyed. Therefore social revolution seems to be the logical consequence of this inhumane system. It becomes clear that there are certain parallels between Marxism and anarchism, but the general argumentation differs. In historical materialism, every new stage of civilization is better than the last one because of the straightening of humanitarian thought and freedom. Such a developing model is rejected by anarchist thinkers. On the other hand, there are axioms that cannot be found in Marxism or in bourgeois thought, such as the idea of the modern military state and the notion that modern civilization has disciplined, not liberated, the social behavior of man.

Anarchist ideas of freedom, nature, and harmony are more comprehensible to large parts of the population than the Marxist philosophy, which is repeatedly based on complicated abstract figures of thought. In anarchism, emotions and sentiments play a huge role; in consequence, art is given a prominent position inside human society.

---

[38] Petr Alekseevich Kropotkin, *Mutual Aid: A Factor of Evolution* (London: n.p., 1902).

Anarchist art literature of the nineteenth century

Based on the definition given in the previous passages, a short list of early examples of anarchist writings on art is presented, some of which might be unknown even to experts in this field. It remains difficult to categorize the texts of the twentieth century, since we cannot call every opposite political direction and every uncommon, liberating, and free thought "anarchist."

One commonly accepted idea is that *Du principe de l'art* (1865) by Proudhon contains traits of anarchist thought. An influence of anarchist thought is perceptible in the writings by some painters who worked in the style of symbolism and pointillism. This is clearly apparent in the correspondence of Camille Pissarro, for instance.[39] At the end of the nineteenth century, the term already had a pejorative meaning because of violent terrorist attacks by anarchist activists. In Italy, Spain, and Germany, anarchist thinking is perceptible in several writings by painters, sculptors, and art theoreticians. Socialism and anarchism in Northern Italy were closely connected.[40] A typical literary document that unconsciously exposes central axioms of anarchism is the essay "Traum eines Arbeiters" (Dream of a Worker) (1893)[41] by Giovanni Segantini. In this vision, a train filled with all classes of society is involved in a horrible accident, but total destruction and chaos enable a new order in which all individuals live in peace and harmony.

The history of German anarchism is a completely neglected theme. Between the 1890s and the 1910s, we can speak of a movement among peasants, agricultural workers, and the petty bourgeoisie in the rural south of the German Reich, especially in the many regions that were not industrialized. One central figure was the writer and politician Gustav Landauer, who predominantly published in socialist magazines since the difference between socialism and anarchism was not very clear even for the editors.[42] His article "Die Zukunft und die Kunst" (Future and Art) (1892)[43] includes all central axioms of anarchist thought, which could easily be confused with the antibourgeois and revolutionary pathos of orthodox Marxism of these years. Landauer categorically rejects all directions of contemporary fine arts; a new art could only grow in the bosom of a new society with liberated individuals.

The best-known anarchist writer, the German anarchist par excellence, is Erich Mühsam, who had been a firm protagonist of the radical bohème,

[39] Timothy J. Clark, *Farewell to an Idea: Episodes from a History of Modernism*, 2nd ed. (New Haven: Yale University Press, 2001), 55–137.

[40] *Radical Light: Italy's Divisionist Painters 1891–1910*, exhib. cat., National Gallery, London, 2008. S. Soldini (ed.), *Addio Lugano bella. Anarchia tra storia e arte*, exhib. cat., Museo d'arte, Mendrisio, 2015.

[41] Giovanni Segantini, "Traum eines Arbeiters" (1893), in Franz Servaes, *Segantini: Sein Leben und Sein Werk* (Leipzig: Klinkhardt & Biermann, 1908). [This text is only included in the extended edition "*Große Ausgabe*" with 263 p., here pp. 70–76.]

[42] Ruth Link-Salinger Hyman, *Gustav Landauer, Philosopher of Utopia* (Indianapolis: Hackett, 1977).

[43] Gustav Landauer, "Die Zukunft und die Kunst," *Neue Zeit* 10, no. 17 (1891): 532–35.

first in Munich and later in Berlin. His satirical style has fascinated many up to the present day. Typical essays by him regarding the arts are "*Der Künstler im Zukunftsstaat*" (The artist in the future state) and "Kollektivität in der Kunst"(Collectivism in art) (1932).[44] The latter article is a sort of retribution for the culture politics of Stalinism.

Anarchism had been mercilessly suppressed in the Soviet Union. All left-wing counter-conceptions to orthodox Marxism had been accused of being "anarchist," often with fatal consequences for the people in charge. In the eyes of Stalinists, all sorts of modern art and literature were influenced by anarchism. It became a catchword without meaning to denounce political opponents of all directions. Thus, it is understandable that after 1945, the category of "anarchism" was avoided in Western social sciences, also since the denunciatory meaning of this term was still in use in the Soviet Union, even in the 1970s.

"Anarchist art theory" is not an established category, even if there is just enough material from the period from 1890 on to construct such a direction. If this category were introduced into art history, it would cause the greatest methodological problems since, in all probability, the whole system of categorizing art of the twentieth century would undergo serious change.

[44] Erich Mühsam, "Der Künstler im Zukunftsstaat," *Die Fackel* 8 (1906); Mühsam, "Kollektivität in der Kunst," *Berliner Tagblatt*, January 26, 1932. Both articles reprinted in Kurt Kreiler, ed., *Fanal. Aufsätze und Gedichte von Erich Mühsam* (Berlin: Wagenbachs Taschenbücher, 1984), 50–58, 179–82.

4.
METHODS

A "method" of analyzing in social sciences has to be comprehensible to others who do not share the world view of the author of a piece of scientific research. It must be possible for another scientist to verify the general argumentation as well as its facts. Marxism in social sciences is not a propagation of certain political content or the preferential treatment of a certain style or artistic direction. Marxist art history is based on different methods. Some of them originate in bourgeois art history but are changed to a large extent, while others are the result of the direct adoption of Marxist philosophy in this special field of historical research. Another question has to be posed: could an art historian revert to the Marxist method without sharing its fundamental convictions? When regarding the definition given above, this might surely be possible, also when one supposes that a great part of Marxist art literature of the second half of the twentieth century borrows some elements of Marxist rhetoric.

Few works were ever published explaining the different methods adopted by Marxist art history. Nicos Hadjinicolaou described only one single method, that of Antal (see chap. 4.1).[1] However, there are alternative methods in the fields of archaeology and art history, three of which are described here (see chap. 4.2–4.4). These are only briefly presented in the following subchapters and expose nothing more than an overall view of the argumentation and application of each method. Generally speaking, Marxist art history is based on positivist studies that aim to uncover the historical facts, usually disguised by bourgeois ideology.

[1] Hadjinicolaou, *Class Struggle*, 95–138.

4.1. THE IDEOLOGY OF THE WORK OF ART

The first method originates directly from an adoption of central axioms of Marxist philosophy. In contrast to the other three methods expounded here, it does not include any element of traditional art history and therefore seems to be the most radical. This method is based on the idea that certain works of art have common visible features (the "style" or other visible signs) and that these common features can be interpreted to be the expression of the ideology of a certain social class. So, if Nicos Hadjinicolaou states, "The ideology of a picture is not its 'content.'"[2]: here the term "ideology" refers to a larger set of thoughts (morals, religious belief, social behavior, etc.) that molds the consciousness of a certain social class and which is also present in the outward appearance of the work of art, or simply put, in the "style".

The relationship between certain social classes and a certain style had already been a matter of consideration in French sociology of art during the nineteenth century (chap. 3.3). The method "ideology of a work of art" is not occupied with the content of a painting or a sculpture, this means with its message which one can understand intellectually; the content of a work of art is on another level of analysis and is not part of this method. But iconography can sometimes helps to uncover the ideology of a work of art. Today, the connection between class ideology and style is even accepted by historians whose view is opposed to Marxism. Regarding this method it is very important to realize that it is not the ideology of a single artist (or of his class) that is expressed in style, but rather the ideology of the social class that commissions or sponsors art, or indeed sometimes the social class intended as recipients. The artist is only the executing instrument of the will of others.

The points of definition are as follows:

- The main question is which social class has commissioned a certain group of works of art with common stylistic features. If there is no information, the visible form of these objects has to be analyzed.
- The general consciousness of this class is mirrored in the "style" of these groups of works. The research is not centered towards the intellectually understandable content of the work, instead research tries to uncover the links between certain social classes and certain works of art. Therefore the word "style" does not have the same semantics as in

[2] Ibid., p. 15.

traditional art history, since the definition and the classification of "style" are radically different.

• To give an overview of all genres of art (including the applied arts) which have evolved during a certain period of time and in a certain geographical region is sufficient to portrait the whole epoch.

• The biography of the artist is never of importance: the work of art first of all depends on the class of commissioners, therefore the style of a work of art does not, or only in a limited sense, mirror the consciousness of the artist's class.

In accordance with the theory of Marx this method refers to the fact that the individual can never break through the barriers of thought set by his own social class, since the subordinated class interests hinder the individual from acting freely (*see* chap. 1.2.). The work of art is created by order of a certain social class, and therefore it mirrors the ideology of this class. The origins of this method lay in the Marxist art exhibitions in the Soviet Union during the 1930s (*see* document 2). *Florentine Painting* (1948)[3] by Frederick Antal and an essay by Nicos Hadjinicolaou (1973)[4] on the stylistic changes visible in the œuvre of Jacques-Louis David are examples of the application of this method.

Visual ideology in German Renaissance art

The following short study is restricted to a few points, such as geographical region (Nuremberg) and point of time (last decade of the fifteenth and first decades of the sixteenth centuries) and a certain genre of art (graphic art). It critically examines whether the idea of Dürer as main Renaissance artist, whose art was popular in all classes of society and was considered to be for all, has a real basis. It discusses what kind of class consciousness is visible in other engravings and single-leaf woodcuts and graphic series by other artists.

The free imperial town of Nuremberg had reached the climax of its economic evolution when it became a main center of trade and manufacture in the fifteenth and sixteenth centuries. In accordance with this, it is a commonly shared opinion that Dürer represents the unsurpassed peak of German Renaissance art. His work does not seem to be centered towards a certain social class, and the various themes and motives of his painting and graphic art appear to have a very different origin of thought. The question remains as to whether there is a common denominator behind his œuvre.

[3] Frederick Antal, *Florentine Painting and Its Social Background* (London: Routledge & Kegan Paul, 1948).

[4] Hadjinicolaou, *Class Struggle*, 107–123.

Pl. 5 Albrecht Dürer, *Peasant Couple Dancing*,
copperplate engraving, 11.8 x 7,5 cm, 1514,
Graphische Sammlung der Universität Erlangen

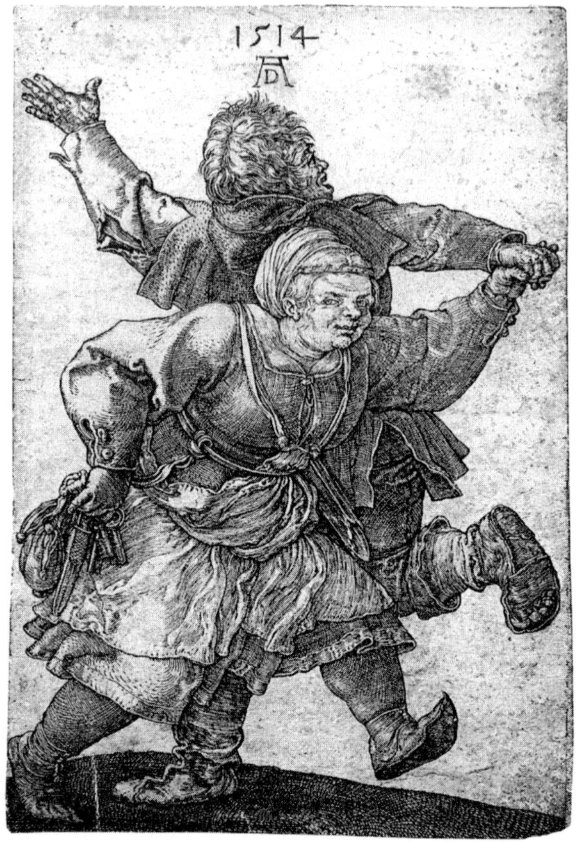

In order to uncover the ideology behind Dürer's art, we have to examine his engraving *Peasant Couple Dancing* (1514) (plate 5). The first element, which is the most striking, is the face of the woman. It is a face far from the ideals of beauty. The same is visible in the proportions of her body. She is stumpy, with short limbs. Her right hand rests on a knife, keys, and a small wallet. That could mean that she is the keeper of the possessions. This observation would tally with the observation that the woman is rendered with masculine traits. Her small face and her huge, fat body indicate her power. In contrast, her husband is a wretched worker. His hair is not cut and is unkempt. His brow is full of wrinkles. A thick eyebrow overshadows the eyes, which he desperately tries to keep open. Perhaps due to his state of drunkenness. His

Pl. 6 Albrecht Dürer, *The Walk*,
copperplate engraving, 19.6 x 12,5 cm, 1496/97,
Kupferstichkabinett, Staatliche Kunsthalle, Karlsruhe

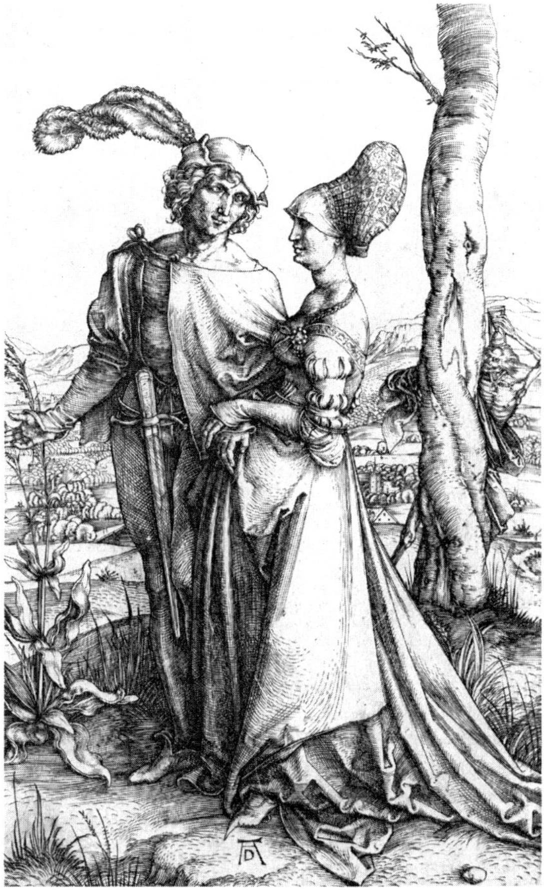

nose is short and his mouth is wide open. The scene as such is certainly dynamic. The couple revolve in an infernal circle. But the scene does not appeal to the sympathy of the observer: we can interpret the scene as a kind of mocking.

An interesting contrast is presented by a copperplate engraving, which today has the title *The Walk* (1496/97) (plate 6). Here we see an urban couple strolling in the countryside. The different iconographic elements of this engraving are of minor importance. The motive is commonly interpreted to show a married wife with her young beau. The figure of death with an hourglass behind the tree trunk would support this idea. The characterization of the couple is, however, of much more significance. The man undoubtedly has harmonious proportions. His stance is reminiscent of the statues of antiquity. The same is the case with the proportions of the woman which correspond with the ideal of beauty of this time. The couple is fashionably dressed and the clothes of the lady lead one to suspect that she belongs to the upper bourgeoisie. In fact, she is not wearing typical German fashion of these years, but her dress seems to be influenced by Venetian fashion. Perhaps, the garments are an indication of the wealth of the city, which was the result, among many other reasons, of trade relations to Italy. The face of the woman, drawn in profile, represents the ideal proportions of antiquity, with a high brow and a straight line of the nose. The gestures of this couple are silent, restrained, and guarded. There is no doubt that here we have representatives of the upper crust.

If the drawing of figures and their suspected social class is compared, it becomes clear that Dürer reserved the harmonious proportion for depictions of representatives of the bourgeois class and sacred figures, whereas figures from the lower classes are characterized by proportions far from antique harmony.

This observation, coupled with many other issues, strengthens the idea that Dürer's art mirrors the ideology of the leading social class, which means the Nuremberg patricians. Around the year 1500, this class consisted of forty-two long-established families which held the majority of thirty-four out of forty-two seats in the Nuremberg town council. If we take into consideration that Nuremberg accepted Luther's Reformation at an early stage, and this step had been accompanied by a certain risk, here we find the key to the interpretation of Dürer's art. Its sometimes ambiguous, undecided, and vague character mirrors the common consciousness of the Nuremberg bourgeoisie in these decades. As the *Peasant Couple Dancing* shows, this art was not conceived for the mass of peasants and artisans, but was exclusively molded by the ideology of the urban bourgeoisie. The modern language of Dürer's art could only be understood inside these circles. During the time of its creation, Dürer's works, such as the *Apocalypse* (1498), remained unintelligible to the mass of population. It is fascinating to interpret the symbols, the imaginary worlds, and the partially violent character of the *Apocalypse* as an echo of the fears, hopes, and beliefs of the Nuremberg patricians. This early urban bourgeoisie was not as elegant and humanistic as propagated by Dürer. But he succeeded in outdoing all his rivals by representing the ideology of this class like no other artist of his time.

Assuming that prints by Dürer represent the visual ideology of the urban bourgeoisie, the question arises as to whether there were any other forms of visual language that corresponded to the visual ideology of other classes of the sixteenth-century society. In this respect, we can compare Dürer's art

Pl. 7 Anonymous artist, *Saint Sebastian and Saint Roch,* single-leaf woodcut, 29.5 x 22 cm, around the 1530s, Graphische Sammlung der Universität Erlangen

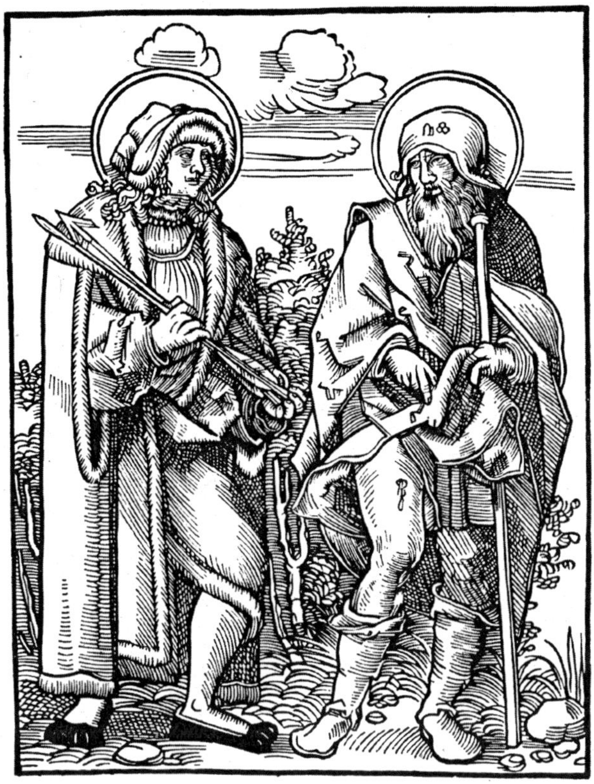

with a single sheet print by an anonymous artist entitled *Saint Sebastian and Saint Roch* (plate 7), which perhaps dates back to the third decade of the sixteenth century.[5] In the twentieth century, the print was attributed to the Nuremberg artist Barthel Beham, but this is quite improbable, since there are no written documents that would confirm such a suspicion.[6] We have

[5] Date according to the depicting technique and Renaissance-like style of the clothes.

[6] The German art historian Heinrich Röttinger attributed some Nuremberg woodblock prints to Barthel Beham in his book *Die Holzschnitte Barthel Behams* (Strassburg: Heitz, 1921), however, these attributions have been discussed and sometimes rejected. The attributions by Röttinger, which were made purely on a stylistic basis, are not convincing. From the late nineteenth century onwards, anonymous prints from Nuremberg graphic artists of the early sixteenth century were already assigned to Sebald and Barthel Beham. Therefore, their work seems to be obscured by these many, often unfounded attributions.

to consider that for the method of interpretation presented here, it is of minor importance to know who executed this or that work of art: the only thing that is important is to identify the class ideology which is mirrored in this work.

So which class ideology is reflected in this print? The scene as such shows a certain simplicity. On the left St. Sebastian is depicted with the instruments of his martyrdom. He appears in the attire of a wealthy burgher. On the right is St. Roch, who points with his forefinger to the plague spot on his thigh. The content of this sheet is clear. However, what might be confusing at first is the archaic style of the print. Its visual language is reminiscent of Gothic woodblock prints. The figures are drawn with a pronouncedly sparse use of artistic means and the represented space appears absolutely flat and stylized. The rendering of the clothes is also reminiscent of the Gothic style, but other elements, such as the primitive *contrapposto* of the figure prove that the print has to be dated in the Renaissance era. Nevertheless, the archaic elements are predominant: St. Sebastian's cape appears as abstract rectangles; his right foot is depicted from a very primitive view. The depiction of archaic elements is not restricted to the figures alone: also the flat rendering of stones, grass, trees and clouds is reminiscent of German woodblock prints of the Gothic age. The logical conclusion would be that the artist did not have the skill to execute a woodblock print in modern fashion, rendered in perspective and with a modern anatomy of the figures. But this suspicion is proved wrong since the anonymous artist shows a certain technical skill and a certain aesthetic feeling.

There are grounds for the suspicion that prints such as *Saint Sebastian and Saint Roch* represent the visual ideology of the large majority of the population, the peasants. Far from education and culture, this majority was still used to an archaic and simple visual language that came from native traditions. The modern Renaissance style was unfamiliar to them and its motives, particularly Greek mythology, were distant from their morals. It was predominantly religious faith that enabled the peasants to bear their situation and preserve a kind of hope.

The astonishing simultaneity of archaic and modern depiction techniques in the art of Nuremberg graphic artists cannot be explained by the slow dissemination of modern techniques or by the skill of artists, even if these factors did certainly play a role. In the explained examples, prints from the same period were executed in a completely different style—but the artist who chose the "primitive" visual language had the same skill and artistic sensitivity as the one who used a more complex and modern visual language. Popular art has reverted for a long period of time to old stylistic forms, since this was a language that was comprehensible to the common people. These simple and often rough kinds of visual expression must be part of art history, since it has to show a representative cross section of all artistic forms of a certain epoch and should not be restricted to some few remarkable works. It should have the aim to expound the whole ensemble of ideological representations of a given period.

4.2. THE MARXIST CONCEPTION OF SOCIAL HISTORY OF ART

The Marxist conception of social history of art is in many ways similar to social history of art taught at the universities; both share the same criteria of research: economic and political history, and the development of depiction techniques (or the evolution of technology in general) are assigned to a certain stage of artistic evolution (*see* chap. 3.2). But there are two differences: Marxist social history is based on Marx's great theories (*see* chap. 1.2. "class theory" and chap. 1.3. "historical materialism"), which is rejected by bourgeois historiography. Marxist social history focuses on certain aspects of culture that do not belong to high culture and which are often ignored or neglected, such as industrial architecture, applied arts, and popular culture. From the second half of the twentieth century onwards, all these forms of aesthetic expression had been the object of a kind of art history guided by purely commercial interests, and therefore a critical reflection is missing.
A short definition of this method contains the following points:

- The Marxist conception of social history is based on political and economic history as well as history of technology, especially of artistic depiction techniques. The evolution of economics and technology automatically causes the rise of certain forms of art. The evolution of artistic forms cannot be isolated from the economic framework.
- The biography of an artist is of lesser importance. If certain biographical facts are used, they serve as an example of the living conditions during a certain epoch.

The first matured and most influential work according to this method is *Art and the Industrial Revolution* (1947)[7] by Klingender. He presented here uncommon forms of art which are normally excluded from the field of aesthetics, such as technical drawings of locomotives from the first half of the nineteenth century and print series on newly opened railway lines in England from the 1830s. A similar work by the same author is the biography *Goya* (1948).[8] From the 1970s on, social history of art met with a certain

---

[7] Francis D. Klingender, *Art and the Industrial Revolution* (London: N. Carrington, 1947).

[8] Francis D. Klingender, *Goya in the Democratic Tradition* (London: Sidgwick & Jackson, 1948).

degree of interest. A recent example is *The Mysticism of Money* (2013)[9] by Andrew Hemingway. Since nearly all modern research on art history contains elements of social history, this indicates a great influence of this methods.

German Rococo and the influence of Enlightenment

After the Thirty Years' War (1618–1648), the German states were in a troubled political and economic situation. Due to the underdeveloped stage of the whole country, the urban bourgeoisie was influenced relatively late by the ideas of the Enlightenment. In its first stage, these new ideas were restricted only to very small circles of writers and scholars, before it also became perceptible among the urban population in the epoch of German rococo (ca. 1710–1760). However, it is a commonly accepted position in German art history that the new emancipatory impulse had no or only a very limited influence on rococo artists.

The following essay examines a particular genre of applied arts: scientific book illustration in the first half of the eighteenth century. In fact, the scientific book illustrators showed great interest in the different directions of emancipatory thought. It is commonly accepted that the whole eighteenth century marks one of the pinnacles of scientific book illustration in Europe. But why?

In the baroque era, the ground for the later development of rococo art was prepared, but the genre of scientific illustration still had a simple character. One example is the engravings contained in *Metamorphosis et historia naturalis insectorum* (1662–1669) by the Dutch painter Johannes Goedaert (or Jan Goedart) (ca. 1617–1668) (plate 8). The illustrations of this work are remarkable for several reasons. They are a stylized rendering of the different stages of the metamorphosis, but show the essential necessary visual information. The purpose of these pictures was not beauty, but the transmission of information. A second aspect seems remarkable. Goedaert did research on the metamorphosis on his own. He was one of the many laymen who undertook investigations in the field of natural science. The borderline between layman and natural scientists had not yet been established then. His skill and technical knowledge of printing techniques enabled Goedaert to visualize the results of his examinations in the field of entomology. This represents a turning away from the common principle of work distinction between natural scientist and graphic artist. From the Renaissance age onwards, scientific book illustration was commissioned by scholars who came from the upper bourgeoisie or aristocracy. The graphic artists

9 Andrew Hemingway, *The Mysticism of Money. Precisionist Painting and Machine Age America* (Pittsburgh: Periscope, 2013).

Pl. 8 Johannes Goedaert,
Metamorphosis et historia naturalis insectorum,
engraving, 15.2 x 10 cm, 1662-69,

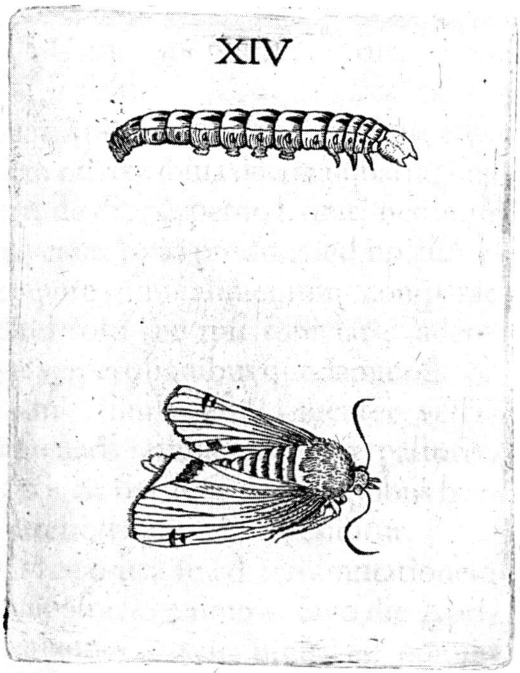

were not, or only in a limited sense, familiar with the plants or animals which they drew on the printing plates. There were different variants of the division of work. Some Italian scientists of the baroque age employed young artists in their own households for several years or even for their entire lives to draw and engrave the pictures that were needed for pictorial explanation of research work. In these cases, the status of the artist was no better than that of a servant. The scientific illustrator was only the executing instrument of the ideas of others. Therefore, the aesthetic quality of scientific drawings and book illustrations of the sixteenth and seventeenth centuries was low in many cases, but its initial aim was to visually transmit the contemporary state of knowledge.

The sudden leap in the quality of scientific book illustration from the late seventeenth century onwards can be explained by two phenomenon: the growing interest of laymen in research work in the fields of botany and entomology and the attempts of artists themselves to be engaged in their own research work. Maria Sibylla Merian (1647–1717) is the most promi-

Pl. 9 Maria Sibylla Merian,
Metamorphosis Insectorum Surinamensium,
colored copperplate engraving, 15.7 x 30.5 cm, 1705,
Niedersächsische Staats- und Universitätsbibliothek Göttingen

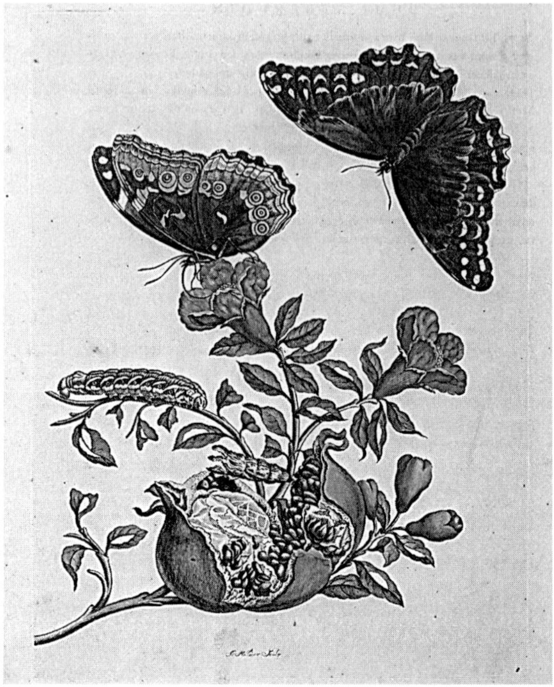

nent example. A copperplate of her book on the metamorphosis of insects in Surinam entitled *Metamorphosis Insectorum Surinamensium* (1705)[10] shows the high aesthetic level of her work (plate 9). She did not depict the different stages of metamorphosis as a succession of different icons isolated from their natural environment but rather assigns certain plants to certain insects. She observed that the different species of caterpillars chose only one or two forage plants. For a better identification of these plants, she depicted them in bloom. It would lead too far to expound every detail of this illustration, but it is clear that there is much more visual information than in Goedaert's pictures. Moreover, the ornamental treatment of forage plants, insect eggs, caterpillars, pupas, and the insects is of high aesthetic value. The most surprising aspect is the rococo style of this illustration,

[10] Merian Sibylla Merian, *Metamorphosis Insectorum Surinamensium, ofte veranderung der Surinaamsche insecten* (Amsterdam: Valck,1705).

Pl. 10 Maria Sibylla Merian,
Lizard, Blue Iguana, Surinam-Ameiva, Gecko,
watercolor painting on vellum, 37.6 x 30.6 cm, ca. 1699-1701,
Archive of the Academy of Sciences, St Petersburg

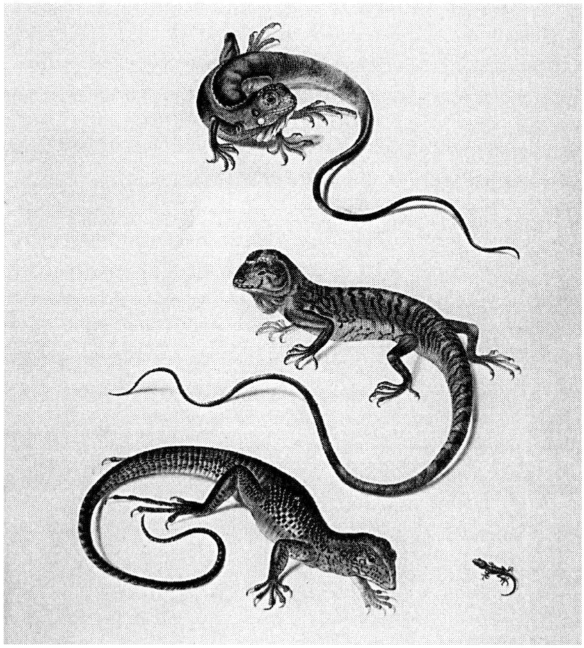

visible in the vivid line of the plants, the decorative rendering of the caterpillars and butterflies, and the pastel-like, very sensitive handmade coloring of the plate. The rococo style is highly emotional. To see it here connected with a picture that is thought to transmit scientific information is something very uncommon. Nevertheless, despite its decorative and aesthetical rendering, the picture conveys the necessary entomological information. Another example from the works of Merian is a fine watercolor painting of different iguanas and a gecko in Surinam (plate 10). It was thought to be a preparatory drawing for a planned book on the animal world in this South American country, which was never executed due to the low number of subscriptions. This picture also shows the rococo style at its best. The iguanas with wave-like tails are ordered like a delicate ornament. The aesthetic quality of this image does not contradict all the requirements of a scientific picture of this period.

One generation after Merian, many artists were already occupied in this field, and the ratio of women is remarkably high. Maria Sibylla Merian had been extremely engaged in her entomological research work. Gifted with an exceptional talent, she learned the technique of copperplate engraving in her stepfather's workshop. This enabled her to engrave her drawings onto the printing plates, to make colored prints, and thus to publish her illustrated books.

In the eighteenth century, scientific illustrators were sometimes called miniature painters, an expression which could cause a certain confusion since this term first of all referred to painters of small portraits in miniature format. August Johann Rösel[11] von Rosenhof (1705–1759) was one of the most remarkable scientific illustrators of this time. Occupied mostly with his own research on insects, spiders, and amphibians,[12] he was also the editor of a monthly journal on entomological research entitled *Monatlich-herausgegebene Insecten-Belustigung* (1740–1761)[13], in which he published his correspondence with other natural scientists and layman researchers all over Europe. This journal prepared the ground for the institutionalization of entomologist research inside the German universities, which took place much later. Rösel's second main work is the *Historia naturalis ranarum nostratium* (1751–58)[14], the *Natural History of Native Frogs* (plate 11). Even for observers familiar with the scientific picture, the plates in Rösel's monograph represent something unusual.

All are molded by the influence of the rococo style, but they originate in the great tradition of anatomical illustration of the baroque epoch, in which the cruelty of dissection was not toned down, but presented in a very naturalistic manner. The frog, which is tied to four pegs, seems to be a horrible motive, but for the observer in the eighteenth century it presented an aesthetic version of anatomical illustration. Even the skeleton of the frog, which seems to be in a lifelike position, is based on the baroque tradition of depicting skeletons in lifelike poses. This plate is marked by a strong influence of the rococo style, which is perceptible in the ornamental treatment of the dissected animal, the composition of the three different motives of the illustration, and the bright pastel, watercolor tones. The discrepancy between aesthetics and scientific demand is toned down. The *History of Native Frogs* was the first illustrated animal monograph of German origin which could enter into competition with the level of scientific book illustration in France and England. Pictures from Rösel's publications served as models in scientific book illustration until the late nineteenth century.

---

[11] The family name is sometimes written as "Roesel."

[12] In Germany, due to the lack of centralised financial state support for scientific research in the fields of zoology, only profound research regarding small, native animals was possible.

[13] August Johann Rösel von Rosenhof, *Der monathlich-herausgegebenen Insecten-Belustigung* [Monthly review, Four Parts], (Nuremberg: author's edition, 1746–1761).

[14] August Johann Rösel von Rosenhof, *Historia naturalis ranarum nostratium. Die natürliche Historie der Frösche* (Nuremberg: Fleischmann, 1753–58).

Pl. 11 August Johann Rösel von Rosenhof,
Historia naturalis ranarum nostratium,
colored copperplate engraving, 155.4 x 35.2 cm, 1751-58,
Universitätsbibliothek Heidelberg

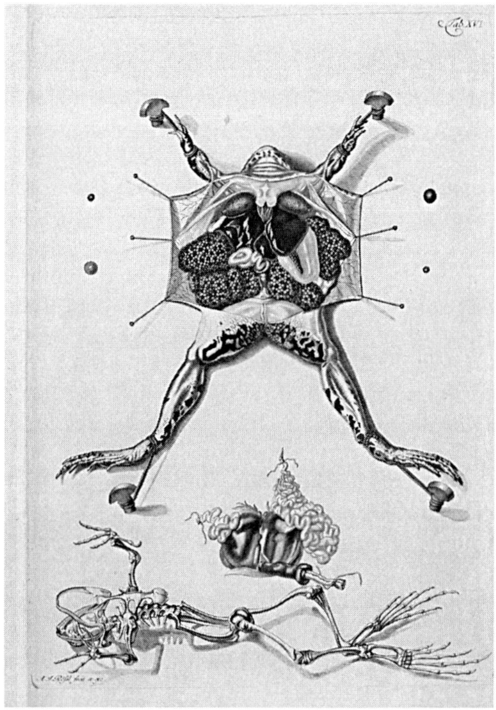

The question arises as to what circumstances gave rise to the engagement of painters and graphic artists regarding the scientific picture—an engagement that far surpassed economic necessity. Some painters became so engrossed in this subject that it led to new discoveries in the fields of zoology and botany. The phenomenon of the "artist-scientist" was born. One can suppose that the impulse for laymen in scientific research was influenced by emancipatory ideas.

Maria Sibylla Merian was a member of the famous Merian family of publishers and topographic illustrators. She belonged to the Frankfurt line of this family and was a trained graphic artist. We know that in the early 1680s, she came under the influence of Pietism. After having joined a Pietist sect in 1686, the founder of which was Jean de Labadie, she, her mother, and her two daughters spent five years living in a Labadist community at Castle Waltha in eastern Friesland. Compared with other women of this epoch, she lived an independent life and therefore she is regarded as a pioneer of early female emancipation.[15] The Labadists were a religious group that exposed a new kind of thought, not identical but parallel to ideas of the early Enlightenment. Belonging to the educated and prosperous classes, the members of this sect showed a certain superciliousness towards other groups. The English philosopher John Locke described in an account written in 1685 the arrogance of the members of this community.

Many educated women were attracted by the sensitive nature of Pietist belief. In the course of the eighteenth century, the connection between Pietism and the erudite woman was the theme of several satirical texts and even of a humorous stage play by the female writer Luise Gottsched, who had been inspired by a similar French piece.[16] Pietist sects like the Labadists offered scholarly women a certain degree of protection as well as a kind of independence and liberty that was suppressed in their own bourgeois families. German literature of the nineteenth and twentieth centuries maintained that Merian had spent her time at Castle Waltha saying prayers and reciting the Bible, though it is more likely that the contrary is true, she could intensify her research work on the metamorphosis of insects, as dated entries in her workbook testify. Even when Pietism had been a religious belief which bestowed great importance to sensitivity and which bears numerous humanistic features, it was neither related to the ideas of Enlightenment nor to the emancipation of women. In its later development, Pietism even began to oppose certain ideas of the Enlightenment. However, this was not the case in Merian's generation.

Some small passages of Merian's work *Metamorphosis Insectorum Surinamensium* (1705) suggest a certain influence of emancipatory ideas which could be interpreted as a reflection of Pietist belief. One example is her criticism of the inhumane living conditions of slaves in this Dutch colony.[17] Other documents she wrote show a self-confident and practical-minded woman, who was extremely engaged in her research work and in business. But there is nearly nothing that goes beyond that. The sometimes perceptible carping—but not criticizing—tone might come from bourgeois utilitarian thought.

---

[15] There is a rich vein of literature on Merian: Natalie Zemon Davis, *Women on the Margins* (Cambridge, MA: Harvard University Press, 1995); Kurt Wettengl, ed., *Maria Sibylla Merian. Künstlerin und Naturforscherin* (Ostfildern: Hatje, 1997); Ella Reitsma, ed., *Maria Sibylla Merian and her Daughters. Women of Art and Science* (Zwolle: Waanders, 2008).

[16] Luise Adelgunde Viktorie Gottsched, *Die Pietisterey im Fischbein-Rocke; oder Die doctormäßige Frau* [Pietism in Fish-Bone Shirt; or The Doctor-like Woman] (Rostock: gedruckt auf Kosten guter Freunde [author's edition], 1736).

[17] Maria Sibylla Merian, *Metamorphosis Insectorum Surinamensium* (Amsterdam: Valck, 1706). [German translation of the Dutch text of this book contained in:] *Metamorphosis Insectorum Surinamensium* [facsimile edn. 1975]. *Beleittext zur Faksimileausgabe nach dem Exemplar der Sächsischen Landesbibliothek Dresden von Helmut Deckert* (Leipzig: Insel-Verlag, 1975), 23 [especially on the slaves].

One generation later, the relationship between rationalistic thought and scientific artists became much clearer, which is reflected in the preface written by Albrecht von Haller (1708–1777) in Rösel's *History of Native Frogs* (1751–1758).[18] Haller was a physician, poet, and main protagonist of the German Enlightenment, and there could be no better proof of the connection between the Enlightenment and visual arts than this preface. In the middle of the eighteenth century in Germany, the debates initiated by the ideas of Enlightenment were not exactly identical with those in France and England. One topic was the political fragmentation of the country into many small and two larger states. For rationalist thinkers, it was clear that this was the reason for the difficult state of economics and underdevelopment. It is not by chance that Haller wrote the preface for Rösel's work, since Haller himself had attempted to establish anatomical book illustration in Germany—an attempt that failed. In Rösel's natural history on frogs, he recognized that, for the first time, a German illustrated publication even surpassed the level of scientific book illustration of the neighboring western countries. In his preface, Haller states that German science and art do not reach the level of other European countries and therefore the German elite would look disdainfully at the products of their own country.[19] But at the same time, he emphasizes the virtues of burghers: diligence, morality, cleanliness, and intelligence. These merits would lead the German people out of their misery.

In the following passages, he criticizes fine arts of his time, which, according to him, were languishing. Consequently, he takes no notice of German architects, painters, and sculptors who are now regarded as the main protagonists of the rococo epoch, but instead lists two artists who are known to a lesser degree in German art history: Johann Daniel Preißler (1666–1737), director of the Nuremberg Academy of Fine Arts, and the botanical artist Georg Dionys Ehret (1708–1770), both influenced by Enlightenment. From the 1730s onwards, ideas of Enlightenment became influential among the educated urban classes. Thus, in the preface of his monograph on frogs, Rösel mentions that one of the aims of his work was to refute the notion among ordinary people that frogs and toads were of devilish origin and were formed out of mud.[20] In many passages of his work he argued against the superstitions of the people and he used his monthly review *Insecten-Belustigung* to fight against traditional views and superstition, which were even commonly held among the educated classes. In this respect, Rösel was a representative of the idea that better education would enable humankind to advance.

[18] Albrecht von Haller, "Vorrede" [1758], in *Natürliche Historie der Frösche*, 1758, p. [v–x].

[19] Ibid., p. [vii].

[20] Ibid., 1 ff.

Jean Le Rond D'Alembert and Georg Christoph Lichtenberg saw modern natural sciences as a central achievement of their epoch. During this period, the phenomenon of the "artist-scientist" came into being. Thus, the scientific picture reached a level that was barely surpassed in later times, since artists undertook scientific research on their own, which enabled them to understand the morphology of plants and the anatomy of animals in detail.

These illustrations are of a remarkable aesthetic quality, but they are also astounding in their scientific precision and their deep understanding of the depicted objects. In the epochs before and also afterwards, painters and graphic artists only had the order to visualize the research work of scientists, and consequently their illustrations did not reflect an intimate knowledge of the represented objects. The astonishing progress of scientific illustration is closely related with the research in natural sciences by laymen, which was promoted by the philosophers of Enlightenment.

Before the Enlightenment, during the baroque epoch, scientific artists only executed the ideas of scholars. Therefore, during this epoch the interest of artists in the further development of scientific illustrations was low. It was not possible for common graphic artists and painters to obtain a higher position within the social hierarchy. The parents of scientific draftsmen of the eighteenth century belonged to the lower petty bourgeoisie and worked in highly specialized professions. They were engravers, musicians at the court, or court gardeners. In this respect, Maria Sibylla Merian was an exception, since she came from a family in the grande bourgeoisie. In the course of the eighteenth century, the petty bourgeoisie, who was open to the ideas of emancipation and freedom of the philosophers of Enlightenment, undertook determined efforts to climb up within the social pyramid, and with this laid the foundations of economic development of the European states.

There were many reasons for the high level of scientific illustration in the first half of the eighteenth century. It would be a nice notion if we were to regard scientific research as the selfless work of individuals with a burning desire to conquer new knowledge and use it for the benefit of mankind. However, this romantic idea does not correspond with reality: the upturn of progress in natural sciences was caused by the huge economic crisis of the late seventeenth and early eighteenth centuries. We know that the population in Western and Central Europe grew, but at the same time it was not possible to increase harvest yields. One of the problems was pests and the destruction of large parts of the harvest by them. Only through a better knowledge of different insects did it become possible to fight against pests. First of all, a categorization of all insects was necessary to determine which ones were harmful. The next step was research on the different states of metamorphosis to find a way to destroy pests. Many articles of Rösel's magazine *Insecten-Belustigung* contain a detailed description of in which state of metamorphosis, where and when the described insects could be culled. Nothing is more misleading than to denote natural sciences of the eighteenth century as a selfless study of nature without any purpose. The work of natural scientists and scientific illustrators of this epoch was not motivated by "love to all of God's creatures" or a "deep respect for nature": it was first of all caused by economic necessity.

4.3. CONTENT AND RECEPTION

The method expounded here has its origins in art criticism championed by the progressive bourgeoisie of the eighteenth and nineteenth centuries. Later Marxist analyses regarding art history are based on these precursory models. The interpretation is based on the "content" of a work of art, meaning its narration, the story which is visible in a painting or in a sculpture. Content can be described and interpreted in very different ways, according to the ideology of the interpreter. Regarding Marxist art history, the original review and reaction during the work's first exhibition constitute important issues. The political orientation of the media and of the author of art criticism is also crucial. All these points allow us to understand the first public reception of a work of art. Later interpretations could also be part of the study, but they should not be mixed with early reviews published at the time of the work of art's first exhibition.

The method "content and reception" is restricted by two points: regarding many periods, we have no reviews or eyewitness reports of the initial reception of a work of art, so the method seems to be limited from the period from the Gothic age onwards. The second point is the restricted political spectrum of publications on art. As a rule, the writers of church institutions and, from the sixteenth century on, authors of the urban bourgeoisie are the main sources.

The content of a work of art can be interpreted very differently. For instance, the many reviews of Delacroix' *Le 28 juillet: la liberté guidant le peuple* (1830) expose the whole political spectrum in post-revolutionary France.[21] Art criticism of the industrialized age amounted to a struggle about the ideological hegemony in visual arts and was partially a substitute for the impossibility of political participation. However, French art criticism is not the only example. The ideological struggle is also apparent in German exhibition reviews of the same period. However, in this case, the dominant ideology was the call for unification, and later, after 1870, the struggle for hegemony in continental Europe. To draw a conclusion: the attempt to

[21] Nicos Hadjinicolaou, *Die Freiheit führt das Volk* (Dresden: Verlag der Kunst, 1991).

uncover the hidden content of a work of art was never an exclusive method of Marxist analysis but is found in all other directions of thought.
A definition of this method includes two points:

- The work of art is at the center of analysis. First of all, the content of a work of art according to its visible signs is described. The social milieu in which the work of art was created, as well as political history, reviews, and all other statements existing at the time of its creation should be part of the interpretation. But analysis is restricted to these points. Other aspects, such as economic history, history of civilization, psychology, etc. are not part of it.
- The Marxist interpretation gives preference to other points than those in bourgeois art history. For instance, the critical, respective socio-critical content of a work of art is esteemed more than aesthetics, innovation, and similar aspects. Therefore, this kind of analysis results in a different system of categorization than in bourgeois art history.

An extreme left-wing or radical interpretation of works of art is not identical to the Marxist method, which is based on historical facts. Even when these facts contradict Marxist hypotheses, they have to be accepted, expounded, and critically discussed. All available historical documents should be analyzed. The results of Marxist analysis cannot be ascertained in advance.

A picture that is not what it ought to be: "The Village Politicians" by Wilhelm Leibl

Today, Wilhelm Leibl (1844–1900) is regarded as a main representative of German realism, but his reputation is very different from that of Gustave Courbet in France. He holds the image as an honest painter of German peasants who was full of idealistic spirit. His painting *Village Politicians* (1876/77) (plate 12) is not very well known, since it is exhibited in a Swiss museum. This work can be taken as an example of how the bourgeois interpretations cover and change the real content of a work of art.

The picture shows five peasants at an inn on Starnberg Lake in the Bavarian countryside near Munich. They are all portrayed from nature. The second man has his head bowed over a paper, which is not easy to identify but which plays a central part in the interpretation of the picture. The two peasants on the right and the one on the left have a stiff position and seem to be distracted by something. Because of the white apron, the person on the left seems to be the landlord, The peasants do not look exhausted, but there is a certain naturalistic trait in this picture that touches even today's observer. The five peasants seem to be studying an old land register, as was suggested by Leibl in a letter to his mother.[22] In this case, the picture would be a photographic-like documentation of an innscene without any deeper meaning.

[22] Letter from Wilhelm Leibl to Gertrud Leibl, dated 3 June, 1876, in *Wilhelm Leibl. Briefe* (Hildesheim: Olms, 1996), 106.

Pl. 12 Wilhelm Leibl, *Village Politicians (Die Dorfpolitiker)*, oil on canvas, 76 x 97.5 cm, 1876-1877, The Oskar Reinhart Foundation, Winterthur

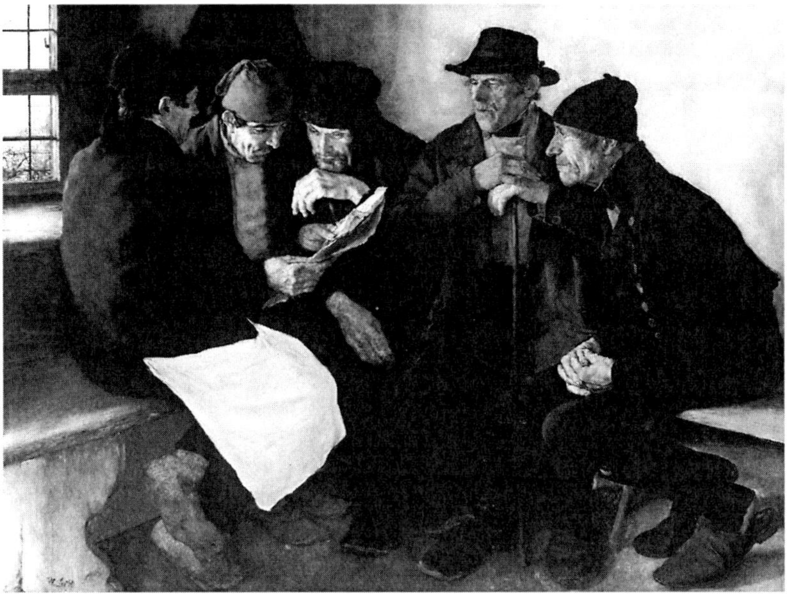

However, the title *Village Politicians* is not the original. It was added later. Perhaps it was chosen because it reflects a kind of petty bourgeois humor. The original title chosen by Leibl for the first exhibition of the picture was *Neueste Nachrichten* (Latest News).

This title had a certain double meaning. It could refer to the only newspaper in Munich with a liberal orientation, the *Neueste Nachrichten*. It stood against the huge majority of other newspapers, which had a conservative and Catholic orientation. Or, the title could refer to the reading of the latest news as such. A similar ambiguous use of newspaper titles can be found in paintings by Courbet. The original title is the key to understanding the picture. If we observe the highly tense posture of the two peasants on the right, we are given the impression that they are listening to something. In accordance with the idea that the scene depicts a peasant reading a newspaper to other peasants, there are two early reviews of this picture, in which both authors describe precisely this situation.[23] Such a scene was uncommon by 1900, but it had been a customary habit in the nineteenth

[23] Karl von Vincenti, "Wiener Briefe LXXV," *Allgemeine Zeitung*, February 4, 1878, no. 35, 306; Ludwig Hevesi, "Feuilleton. Künstlerhaus," *Fremden-Blatt* (Vienna), January 12, 1878, no. 12, 11–12.

century when the great majority of Bavarian peasants had no or only rudimentary knowledge of reading and writing due to the poor state of primary education there. In contrast to the industrialized regions in the north and west of Germany, the south remained in an underdeveloped state. The picture is a telling—but perhaps unintentional—documentation of this situation.

What were the first reactions to this picture? The picture was conceived by Leibl to attract a larger audience at the great exhibitions of this epoch, it should be sold for a high price to a renowned collector, and thus elevate the renown of the artist. Therefore, the picture was first exhibited in December 1877 at the Art Society in Munich and in January 1878 at the House of Artists in Vienna and later the same year, at the World Fair in Paris. We have only seven known exhibition reviews from this period. All reviews appeared in publications that hold a firm bourgeois political standpoint, such as the German magazine *Kunstchronik*, the newspapers *Allgemeine Zeitung*, *Fremden-Blatt*, and the French journals *Gazette des Beaux-Arts*, and *L'Art*.

The *Kunstchronik* was a supplement in the most renowned art historical magazine *Zeitschrift für bildende Kunst*. In the 1870s, its contributors oscillated between a liberal and a nationalistic conservative position. In the *Allgemeine Zeitung*, the most important newspaper in the south, exhibition reviews showed a strong conservative and nationalistic standpoint. Formerly, in the 1850s, the position of its main critic, Friedrich Pecht, had adopted a more liberal position. The Vienna-based *Fremden-Blatt* defended the position of the liberal bourgeoisie. Its art critic Ludwig Hevesi showed a strong orientation towards French culture. This was the spectrum of opinions possible in the German-speaking countries. The year 1878 had seen the adoption of Bismarck's anti-socialist laws: therefore the standpoint of the petty bourgeoisie and the Socialists is missing. However, German art criticism of these years cannot be understood in its entirety if the influence of the French press and of French authors is left out. It is astonishing that French authors who hold left-wing positions, like Théophile Thoré, were able to publish articles in the German press. At the same time, the French press reviewed German art in light of the struggle for cultural hegemony in Europe between the two nations. This might be the reason that we have exhibition reviews of the *Village Politicians* in French magazines such as *Le Figaro*, the *Gazette des Beaux-Arts* and *L'Art*. One was written by Edmond Duranty, a representative of the once revolutionary petty bourgeoisie.

If we analyze the first three exhibition reviews of 1878 by German authors, these establish a relationship between Courbet and Leibl.[24] The

[24] R. [anonymous author], "Münchener Kunstverein," *Kunstchronik. Beiblatt zur Zeitschrift für bildende Kunst*, 13 (1878), column 245; Karl v. Vincenti, *Wiener Briefe* (1878); Ludwig von Hevesi, *Feuilleton. Künstlerhaus* (1878).

latter is characterized as portraying "ugliness," but with this, he is near to "truth." It is interesting that all three early exhibition reviews do not speak unfavorably of his picture and call it a progression in the further development of German genre painting. During the Paris World Fair, even the influential conservative critic Friedrich Pecht changed his opinion of Leibl's art. He avoided mentioning the relationship to Courbet but emphasized the Old Master qualities of the *Village Politicians* and referred to it as "Holbein-style,"[25] which means the painting style of the German Renaissance. Hans Holbein the Younger was held in high esteem by the German bourgeois of the nineteenth century. With the positive review by Pecht a total shift of the reception of Leibl's work becomes visible.

The French reviews published during the Paris World Fair interpreted Leibl's change from another angle. Even when all known French reviews still described Leibl's *Paysans* (the new title given to the picture on the occasion of the Paris World Fair) with the same words as Courbet's realism had been characterized before, the reviewers recognized a new trait in this sort of realism: the painstaking imitation of nature with some elements reminiscent of German Renaissance painting.[26] The German as well as the French reviewers all spoke in favor of the picture, but the reasons and arguments for this contrasted greatly between the two fractions. Some months before, at the exhibition in Vienna in 1878, Ludwig von Hevesi summarized the intentions of the artist in a succinct manner:

> Leibl is the sans-culotte of Realism. He knows only one art: nature. He strives to represent its outward appearances, like it is in its naked and ordinary reality, in its whole inexorable truth. The obliteration of idealism is his ideal. An artist who adopts this extreme standpoint, must, in the course of time, necessarily go beyond any extreme. . . . Leibl in particular likes painting the ugly. He becomes immersed in it with unparalleled love and joy, he is enthused by rationality anddelights in the repulsive.[27]

Within the context of German art criticism of the 1870s—German art critics mostly exposed idealistic praise or humorous mocking of certain artists and styles—the tone of this review was very unusual. It is reminiscent of

[25] Friedrich Pecht, "Deutsche Briefe über die Pariser Weltausstellung," *Beilage zur Allgemeinen Zeitung*, May 29, 1878, no. 149, 2194.

[26] Edmond Duranty, "Les écoles étrangères de peinture I," *Gazette des Beaux-Arts* 20 (1878), 60–62. Charles Tardieu, "La peinture a l'exposition universelle de 1878," *L'Art* 2 (1879), 83–85.

[27] Ludwig von Hevesi, *Feuilleton* (1878), 11: "Leibl ist der Sansculotte des Realismus. Er kennt nur eine Kunst: die Natur. Die Erscheinungen derselben wiederzugeben, wie sie in der nackten, gemeinen Wirklichkeit dastehen, in ihrer ganzen unerbittlichen Wahrheit, das ist sein Streben. Die Ausrottung des Idealen ist sein Ideal. Ein Künstler, der auf diesem äußersten Standpunkt steht, muß mit der Zeit nothwendig über das Aeußerste hinausgehen. [...]. Und so malt Leibl mit Vorliebe das Häßliche. Er versenkt sich darein mit einer Liebe und Freude ohne Gleichen, er schwärmt für das Nüchterne und ist entzückt von dem Abstoßenden."

similar reviews by Théophile Gautier and other liberal authors regarding the exhibition of Courbet's paintings at the Paris Salon of 1850-1851. Here, we find the same topics: the painter as a revolutionary, as a destroyer of idealism, as a tremendous imitator of nature, as a lover of untarnished ugliness, etc.[28] But this conception of realism met with heavy opposition in view of growing nationalism and the rejection of modern French culture in the German Reich. We must pay attention to the fact that the aforementioned review by Hevesi was published in an Austrian newspaper. The Austro-Hungarian Empire was open to the influence of French culture, in contrast to Bismarck's German Reich, where huge efforts were made to establish a counter-model against the French influence. "Idealistic realism" ("*Ideal-realismus*") and "German realism" ("*deutscher Realismus*") were promoted to combat French realism, in painting as well as in literature. In the light of this, it becomes clear that any attempt to adopt Courbet's realism was destined to fail. Therefore, if we examine the picture more closely, it is not the naturalistic depiction of the five men, but the situation as such—the reading of news to an audience of illiterates of the lowest class—that constituted a very uncommon theme in German painting.

What is the ideology behind this painting? Is it similar to Courbet's realism? The biography of Leibl would speak against this. The painter came from a conservative petty bourgeois family. His father had been employed as a musician by the Catholic church in his native city of Cologne. His parents sent him to Munich, even though Leibl would have liked to study at the Academy of Fine Arts in Dusseldorf, but his parents imagined him safely away from liberal influences in the provincial narrowness of the capital of the Bavarian kingdom. Leibl's letters to his mother, upon whom he was financially dependent, indicate that the artist himself was deeply molded by idealistic thinking, even when a materialistic undertone is sometimes evident. Undoubtedly, Leibl was distanced from politics; his life was devoted to art, predominantly his own art. He had astonishing self-confidence. In the late 1870s, he left his former ideals behind and adopted a more conservative attitude, due to the poor state of his finances.

As a student in the early 1870s, he stood under the influence of liberal thought, mostly identical with the view of other students at the academy. Leibl's letters, as well as accounts by friends, prevent him from being categorized as an intellectual or even a critical artist. When taking this fact into account, how can the pictures of the 1870s be interpreted? From the late 1860s until the late 1870s, he was unable to find a supporting social class willing to be the patrons of his art. His genre paintings of the 1870s were not commissioned. But the artist hoped to find buyers at great art exhibitions; perhaps he hoped for the liberal industrial bourgeoisie, which

[28] Théophile Gautier, "Salon de 1850–51. M. Courbet," *La Presse, Feuilleton* (Paris), February 15, 1850.

did not exist in the underdeveloped rural south of Germany. The Bavarian king and aristocracy still played the main role as patrons of art. The urban bourgeoisie was molded by conservatism. The idea of adopting Courbet's realism in this kind of society was a very strange idea for a young artist who did not know this region very well. There was no market for Courbet's realism in the south. It had been an American collector, Steward, who acquired *The Village Politicians*, and it was only much later that it was sold to a Swiss collector. The pictures of the 1870s could not be sold, because the class that would have shared its progressive conception did not exist. Therefore, around 1877/78, Leibl changed to the Holbein-style, an old-fashioned way of painting, which guaranteed him certain success among the Catholic aristocracy of the Bavarian countryside. After 1878, his fame began to grow for a short period, since his Old Master style, reminiscent of the German Renaissance, fitted with the idea of a genuine German realism free of French influence. Leibl lost interest in a further continuation of a Courbet-like style and changed to arch-conservative circles.

The question remains as to how the few genre paintings between 1874 and 1878 could be interpreted. The painter did not have any critical intention. It is more the depiction technique, the presentation of the real, the style of Courbet's realism, that enabled the painter to include particles of reality, surely unconsciously, in his pictures. Leibl was possessed by the idea of "truth", and therefore he portrayed the depressing situation of the Bavarian peasantry as a neutral observer. The picture gives the impression of a dull and archaic society, which had been left untouched by progress. If we consider that Courbet's *Stonebreakers* can be interpreted as an advanced stage of realism in visual arts—without an open and emotional social charge but with an unprecedented observation of ordinary, contemporary society—twenty years later, the same kind of observation can be found in certain works by Wilhelm Leibl. In this respect, an anonymous review of 1878 about the *Village Politicians* had not lost its validity: "Since Courbet's celebrated *Stonebreakers,* nothing similar seems to have been created."[29]

[29] R. [anonymous author], "Münchener Kunstverein," *Kunstchronik* 13 (1878), column 245: "Seit Courbet's berühmten *Steinklopfern* ist vielleicht nichts Aehnliches mehr geschaffen worden."

4.4. HISTORICAL MATERIALISM AND ART HISTORY

O

If Marx's conception of history is connected with art history, the results of research and interpretation will be very different from those investigations based on bourgeois thought (*see* chap. 1.3. "historical materialism"). Interpreting human history as a steadily upward climbing line, historical materialism is different to all other conceptions of history, for instance those that presume a wave-like evolution or those that are convinced of an unstructured course of history.

The vision of human history conceived by Marx stood in contradiction to the majority of concepts that were then in use in the historiographical sciences. For instance, in bourgeois art history of the nineteenth century, the Graeco-Roman epoch was seen as the climax of humanity and culture, whereas the Middle Ages were interpreted as the "dark age". Marx turned this system upside down by stating that the Graeco-Roman epoch had been a primitive state of civilization: only a small group, the oligarchy, at the top of the social pyramid had access to literature and the arts. The culture of Greece and the later Roman Empire was based on the work of slaves, who worked under inhumane conditions. The Middle Ages represented progress, since the social situation, even that of the serfs, had been much better than that of the slaves of antiquity. The culture of the Middle Ages was based on a higher developed stage of economics, encouraged by new technical inventions, and supported by a new social structure. The rise of early capitalist economies in urban city-states logically open a new historical period, which resulted in fully developed capitalist economies and the industrial civilization which represents the hitherto reached climax of culture. The present stage will only be surpassed by a new form of economics and civilization in the communist society. This is, in short, the general vision of historical materialism which has revolutionized the conception of human history. It took a very long time before elements of historical materialism were introduced into social sciences at universities, but in the second half of the twentieth century, bourgeois historiography adopted large parts of it.

This adoption bears several consequences. Historical evolution is explained through its breaks: Marxist history is focused to a far larger extent on sociological changes and revolutions than other directions of history writing. Each of these breaks signals another stage of historical evolution. For instance, the French Revolution of 1789 was a main focus of research. Marxist history interprets human history as a succession of different epochs, each of which marks another stage in an upward-climbing process.

However, already bourgeois historiography from the early nineteenth century onwards had used similar terminology. For instance, authors whose ideology was fixed on extreme conservative or nationalistic thought also characterized medieval society as "feudalism" and contrasted it with "modern bourgeois society". Sometimes the only difference between the progressive historiography of the twentieth century and Marxist history writing is that latter refers to class theory and has as its vision a future classless society.

Elements of historical materialism can be found in the works of all Marxist art historians and nearly all left-wing art historians of the twentieth century, albeit in a very subtle and highly developed manner. An example is the work of Meyer Schapiro concerning several questions about the art of the early Christian epoch and Medieval art included in his *Selected Papers* (1977–1999).[30] Another example are publications by Robert Sukale.[31] Especially in the periods from early Christianity until modern times, a Marxist analysis can bring astonishing results. These periods had almost exclusively been a matter of art historical research at the universities, and the ideological layers built upon these epochs thus seem to be firmly fixed and unchangeable.

The Gothic canon of human body proportions

Regarding art historical classification systems on rules of human proportions, the essay "The History of the Theory of Human Proportions" (1921/1955)[32] by Erwin Panofsky remains one of the most important reference texts. Its general argumentation, presented with great eloquence and certainty, was never called into question. This essay, which was reworked by the author during his exile in New York, has influenced the view on the history of canons in Germany as well as in the Anglophone world. However, many of its conclusions are based on erroneous observations and thus lead up a blind alley.

In the following lines, it is not possible to present anything more than a brief critique of this theory on the evolution of canons. Panofsky described

---

30 See especially: Meyer Schapiro, *Romanesque Art* (New York: Braziller, 1977); *Late Antique, Early Christian and Mediaeval Art* (New York: Braziller, 1979).

31 Robert Sukale, "Thesen zum Bedeutungswandel der Fensterrose," in *Bauwerk und Bildwerk im Hochmittelalter*, ed. by Karl Clausberg (Gießen: Anabas-Verlag, 1981), 259–294.

32 The American translation of 1955 constitutes the basis of this essay ("The history of the theory of human proportions as a reflection of the history of styles," in Erwin Panofsky, *Meaning in the Visual Arts* (Garden City, New York: Doubleday, 1955), 55–107). There are different versions of this article. Panofsky tried to establish a new terminology for the categorization of historical canons, which makes a critical discussion of this text very difficult, since the first German version of 1921 differs in parts from later translations ("Die Entwicklung der Proportionslehre als Abbild der Stilentwicklung," *Monatshefte für Baukunst und Städtebau* 14 (1921): 188–219). Panofsky's own American translation of 1955 presents a developed and a mature form of his article.

five different systems: the method of drawing the human body by the Egyptians, the anthropometrical of the Greeks, the Byzantine canons, the Gothic system, and, finally, the theory of proportions created in the Renaissance era.

Panofsky established two great systems of canons of proportions: the "technical system" and the "objective system" (or "anthropometrical system") of proportions.

The technical system refers to a given unit (for instance, a foot length or an abstract measurement), which is used to construct a grid net. In this grid net the figure is drawn: thus, the "technical system" means that the human figure is drawn in a rigid system of lines constructed with the help of one given unit. The figure can be drawn in a naturalistic manner, but only in stereotypical postures, such as the front or profile view. The geometrical grid system in which the figure is drawn has no organic relationship to the real proportions and the anatomy of the figure. The nature of this system is "technical."

In the "objective system," a unit of measurement is also used, but there is no geometrical grid. The unit (for instance, the height of the face) serves to define the dimensions of other parts of the body, in many cases as a fractional number of the given unit: for instance, the forearm has the length of one and a half units. Therefore, figures can be rendered more organically and it became possible to depict and sculpt them in different stances and even in movement. Thus, the very nature of this system is "objective" or "anthropometric".

This division into two great systems as such has to be criticized: all historically documented canons for drawing the human figure are, in fact, based on a unit of measurement and on a geometrical basic construction. But this is not the place to criticize and to disprove the theory on the evolution of canons expounded by Panofsky in all details. Here, only the example of the Gothic canon is discussed critically.

According to Panofsky, in Egyptian art, the "technical" and "objective" system of proportions coincide with each other[33], in contrast to Greek art, which "has free[d] itself completely from the Egyptian system of proportions." Panofsky states that Egyptian art is in "a sphere of magical reality," whereas for "the Greeks, the work of art exists in a sphere of aesthetic ideality."[34] Panofsky admires the proportions of the human figure in Classical Greek art and its canons are praised as the first peak of the evolution. Belonging to the "objective" system of proportions, the canons of antiquity had an anthropometric character. It became possible to depict the human body in movement and in foreshortenings. Panofsky informs the reader, however, that there are few texts of antiquity in which canons of human

---

[33] Panofsky, *Meaning*, 57.

[34] Ibid, 61–62.

body proportions are described. The most important source is a short passage in *De architectura libri decem*[35] by Vitruvius. Panofsky's remarks about the nature of the canons of antiquity are thus lack real foundation, and some are, indeed, only of hypothetical nature.

Panofsky states that the canons of the Byzantine and the following Gothic epoch had opened a new stage of the evolution, since they relieved those of antiquity. These new canons exposed a geometrical and two-dimensional character. Byzantine and Medieval art had conserved elements of the three-dimensionality of antiquity in a misleading manner: perspective is presented in a stiff form and the whole rendering does not create the illusion of depth. Because the classical canons fell into oblivion, the canons of Gothic art signified the greatest possible distance from anthropometric systems of Greek classical art. After Panofsky, the Gothic system has absolutely nothing in common with the measurement of the body, as he explained using the example of the illustrations in the lodge book (ca. 1225–1235) of the French architect Villard de Honnecourt:

> Here the figure is no longer "measured" at all, not even according to head- or face-lengths; the schema almost completely renounced, so to speak, the object. The system of lines—often conceived from a purely ornamental point of view and at times quite comparable to the shapes of Gothic tracery—is superimposed upon the human form like an independent wire framework.[36]

He develops his argumentation through the study of a sketch of a male figure which is known as "front figure" (plate 13) of the lodge book (on the right side of this sheet). To quote Panofsky again: "Thus the upright male figure ... results from a construction that has absolutely no relation to the organic structure of the body ...[37] Panofsky concludes that Gothic art was exclusively concerned with the geometrical schematization of the dimensions of the human body, contrasting with this with the anthropometrical canons of antiquity. According to him, the Gothic canons were far from nature, and represented a metaphysical interpretation of proportions of animals and human beings.

Panofsky draws the conclusion that is was not before the Renaissance and the rediscovery of anthropometry that the organic representation of the body marked a return to the Greek and Roman tradition. Painters began to search for a new harmony. The Renaissance saw the return of the anthropometric canons and Dürer's measurements and publication of his *Four Books* in 1528 "marks the climax which the theory of proportions had never reached before nor was to reach ever after."[38] So, in the eyes of

[35] Vitruvius, *Vitruvii de architectura libri decem* [tansl. by C. Fensterbusch] (Darmstadt: Wissenschaftliche Buchgesellschaft Darmstadt, 1964).

[36] Panofsky, *Meaning*, 83.

[37] Ibid.

[38] Ibid, 103–104.

Pl. 13 Lodge book of Villard de Honnecourt,
Page with proportion diagrams of the figure,
pen and ink drawing on vellum, ca. 24.6 x 15.2 cm, ca. 1225-1235,
Bibliothèque Nationale de France, Paris

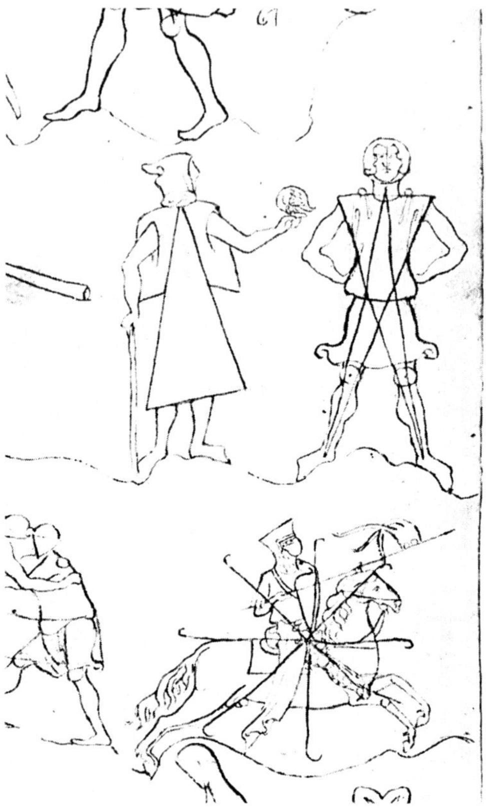

Panofsky, after Dürer a steady and unstoppable decline of the theory of proportions took place.

His thesis on the evolution of canons is adapted perfectly to the traditional model of bourgeois art history of the nineteenth century: Greek classical art is esteemed above all and is regarded as an unsurpassable model marking the first peak of a tradition which had been forgotten in medieval art. The Middle Ages were a spiritual age and therefore figures had a purely ornamental and religious function and were far from the model of nature. In contrast to this, the Renaissance is regarded as a sudden new peak in the evolution: the harmony of classical Greek art was established again.

Pl. 14 Assumed construction of the 'front figure' by Villard de Honnecourt

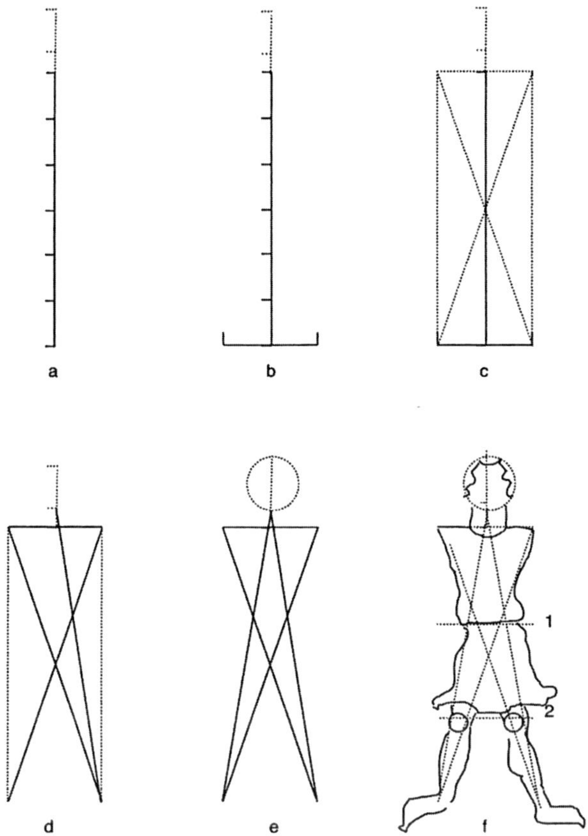

The question is whether Panofsky's thesis on the evolution of canons is right. Do the examples he mentions really support his thesis? Sheet 37 of the lodge book of Villard de Honnecourt has to be examined again (plates 13 and 14). At first glance, for an observer unfamiliar with drawing and the practical use of proportion schemes, the sheet seems to depict abstract figures such as a pentagram, squares, circular arcs, triangles, etc. In these geometrical forms, the figures are rendered more or less organically. A key to understanding the construction is the so-called "front figure", which has also been described by Panofsky in detail. It seems to be of central importance to understanding the whole system. Panofsky saw only two vertically elongated triangles, or rather he interpreted the basic linear drawing as a kind of pentagram. In this, the figure was drawn un-organically and without referring to the traditional canons of antiquity.

First of all, we have to ask what the purpose of figures like these was. It is well expounded in modern secondary literature that they served as models for glass windows, manuscripts illumination, mural paintings, or in relief sculpture and other forms of art. The instruments of the artisans of the Gothic epoch were not highly developed. To draw lines of a surface, they used a kind of ruler (but without a subdivision into smaller parts of measurement), a string and chalk. There was no commonly accepted and exact system of measurement, such as the metering rule of the industrial age. Therefore, all subdivisions of lines had to be constructed.

The function of the front figure was to put a figure in a determined size onto a given surface. Its size could be very small (book illumination) or large (glass windows). A highly complicated construction would not have been of benefit for practical application. Smaller figures could be drawn freely into these two elongated triangles, without any supporting construction. But if one tries to render the figure on a larger scale, it becomes necessary to draw a vertical line (plate 14a). In the diagram shown here, this vertical line is subdivided into six equal lengths. We can call one of these parts a modulus or unit. The dotted line, which was not part of the first basic construction, shows that the head has the length of one unit and the neck has the length of half a unit. Together, the figure has the height of seven and a half models. If we take into account that the length of one model is exactly the same length as the head in front view, the whole figure is in accordance with a common canon from antiquity with seven and a half lengths.

Next, two of the units serve to define the breadth of the figure (plate 14b). This is also similar to a canon that was used much later in the Renaissance era, where the shoulders had the breadth of two head lengths. The third step was the construction of an elongated square, whose opposite corners are connected with a line (plate 14c). If two further lines from the lower corners are drawn to the middle line exactly to the point where the half modulus of the neck ends (plate 14d), a pentagram-like figure emerges (plate 14e). A circle marks the position of the head. The diameter of this circle corresponds with one modulus. Thus, the height of the figure corresponds to seven and a half head-lengths. Like in antiquity, the unit of measurement is the head or the face. Once the two triangles are drawn, which are the basis of the whole construction, the figure could be drawn freely into this linear structure (plate 14f). The construction reveals several other interesting aspects: almost at the point where the two triangles cross each other, the lower end of the trunk is positioned (plate 14f 1). There are two small circles for the knees inside the lower top of the triangles, approximately at the end of the second modulus length (plate 14f 2). Not before the whole construction was finished, the detail of the head was drawn. Again, as the diagram proves, the height of the male figure is seven and a half heads-lengths, corresponding to the diagrams on proportions of the Renaissance.

The "front figure" by Villard bears a very special function: it should be remembered that this figure is part of a lodge book of an architect. As logical consequence, it served for practical purposes, such as the transfer of a small sketch to a size which was needed to integrate figurative sculptures and mural paintings in the architecture of a building.

The Gothic canon does not represent a primitive or low state in the evolution of the theory of proportions, and in no way does it constitute a decline in comparison with the canons of antiquity. Its linear schemata signify a metaphysical symbolism only in a limited sense. As expounded in visual diagrams in the lodge book by Villard de Honnecourt, the Gothic canon was a highly evaluated system of depicting the human body in the right proportions. This lodge book shows a far greater complexity and technical knowledge than those of the Graeco-Roman period. Standing between the antique tradition and the Renaissance theory of proportions, some sketches of the lodge book prepared the foundations of the fifteenth century. However, Panofsky is right when he states that the diagrams of the lodge books do not have the complexity of those of Leonardo da Vinci. It must be called into question whether the linear schemes in Villard's chapter on *portraiture* originate in metaphysical thought or religious symbolism. The contrary is the case: these diagrams served a practical use regarding the embellishment of architecture. The front figure belongs to diagrams on human proportions, but it was a technical mechanism for scaling a figure in any height needed. The nature of diagrams like these is matter-of-fact and functional.

Establishing a link between the Graeco-Roman tradition and that of the Renaissance, the Gothic canon of proportions represents an advance compared with antiquity. As a consequence, the whole system of categorization established by Panofsky must be drawn into question. His strict subdivision into "technical" and "objective" canons must also be critically discussed, since ancient canons of human body proportions were closely related to those of following epochs. Panofsky exposes observations that are correct, but his system of categorization as such—the wave-like succession of art historical epochs—is surely unrealistic. Likewise, his conviction that the *Vier Bücher von menschlicher Proportion* by Dürer represented the climax of theory of proportions which was never reached afterwards does not seem very well-founded. Dürer's theory of proportions really does not mark the climax of this evolution; his *Four Books* correspond with the Mannerist theorization typical of the sixteenth century. It was not before the mid nineteenth century that the evolution of the theory of proportions came into a phase of stagnation.

Even the general idea of a history of the theory of proportions as a reflection of the history of styles is wrong. The theory of proportions is a technique for the depiction of the figure that changed during the course of centuries, but it represents a continuous tradition from antiquity until the present time. As a technique of artistic representation, the canon of proportions has something to do with style, but to a lesser degree than

Panofsky stated. The "style" has been influenced to a much larger degree by other components, such as the general evolution of depiction techniques and the demands of society.

EPILOGUE

The frontispiece of this book is a very special work of art. It is an engraving by Sebald Beham of 1544, which, from the nineteenth century onwards, had the title *Fähnrich und Trommler* (*Standard-Bearer and Drummer*). It is found under this title in the catalogue raisonné des œuvres (1901)[1] compiled by the German art historian Gustav Pauli, who is regarded as one of the great German art historians. The title *Standard-Bearer and Drummer* was adopted in nearly all following publications[2], even when there is another modern title sometimes used: *Acker Contz and Klos Wuczer*. Considered against this background, this engraving shows one of the common scenes with a lansquenet and a peasant soldier, figures that were popular during the late Renaissance era. It is only one of approximately 1,200 engravings in Pauli's general catalogue of works. Accordingly, it seems to represent nothing special. However, a closer inspection very quickly reveals that the picture had another title during the time of its print. In the right corner of the etching one can clearly read IM BAVEREN KRIEG 1525 (In the Peasants' War 1525). In this respect, the picture shows something completely different to what is suggested by bourgeois art history: it shows a scene from the German peasant war of 1525 in a certain heroic manner. It is suspected that Sebald Beham and his brother Barthel Beham sympathized with the peasants, so it is more likely that this etching was conceived as a memorial of this short and tragic uprising of the people.

During the past and in the present, art history has almost exclusively been a matter of bourgeois research, so that the ideological layers upon the epochs of art seem to be firmly fixed and unchangeable. Western art history is not even connected with the different conceptions of political history. It represents a sort of idealized and wistful historiography in which the desires and ideological aims of bourgeoisie are presented as a "scientific history" of aesthetic forms.

1 Gustav Pauli, *Hans Sebald Beham. Ein kritisches Verzeichnis seiner Kupferstiche, Radierungen und Holzschnitte* (Straßburg: Heitz, 1901), 203–204 (no. 202).

2 For example: Friedrich W. H. Hollstein, *German Engravings, Etchings and Woodcuts ca. 1400–1700*, volume 2 (Amsterdam: Menno Hertzberger, 1954), 144.

Like every school of thought, Marxism can be interpreted in different ways and consequently it has been subject of many transformations during the course of its evolution. But two traits distinguish the philosophy of Karl Marx from all others. First of all, he re-addressed the foundations and ideas of the philosophers of Enlightenment and adapted these to the new age of industrialization. Marx recognized the nature of this new epoch in a clear manner, better than the philosophers of the present time, since he had knowledge of the pre-industrialized epoch before and therefore perfectly understood the break. Finally, Marxism is a political philosophy that aims to transform human society into a community which offers every single human being the same opportunities and in which the state assumes the role of the fair distribution of labor and the means of production.

APPENDIX

DOCUMENT 1

Karl Marx, *A Contribution to the Critique of Political Economy* [extract from the preface], 1859, in MECW 29, 263–264.

"In the social production of their existence, men inevitably enter into definite relations, which are independent of their will, namely relations of production appropriate to a given stage in the development of material forces of production. The totality of these relations of production constitutes the economic structure of society, the real foundation, on which arises a legal and political superstructure and to which correspond definite forms of social consciousness. The mode of production of material life conditions the general process of social, political and intellectual life. It is not the consciousness of men that determines their existence, but their social existence that determines their consciousness. At a certain stage of development, the material productive forces of society come into conflict with the existing relations of production or—this merely expresses the same thing in legal terms—with the property relations within the framework of which they have operated hitherto. From forms of development of the productive forces these relations turn into their fetters. Then begins an era of social revolution. The changes in the economic foundation lead sooner or later to the transformation of the whole immense superstructure. In studying such transformations it is always necessary to distinguish between the material transformation of the economic conditions of production, which can be determined with the precision of natural science, and the legal, political, religious, artistic or philosophic—in short, ideological forms in which men become conscious of this conflict and fight it out. Just as one does not judge an individual by what he thinks about himself, so one cannot judge such a period of transformation by its consciousness, but, on the contrary, this consciousness must be explained from the contradictions of material life, from the conflict existing between the social forces of production and the relations of production. No social formation is ever destroyed before all the productive forces for which it is sufficient have been developed, and new superior relations of production never replace older ones before the material conditions for their existence have matured within the framework of the old society. Mankind thus inevitably sets itself only such tasks as it is able to solve, since closer examination will always show that the problem itself arises only when the material conditions for its solution are already present or at least in the course of formation. In broad outline, the Asiatic, ancient, feudal and modern bourgeois modes of production may be designated as epochs marking progress in the economic development of society. The bourgeois relations of production are the last antagonistic form of the social process of production—antagonistic not in the sense of individual antagonism but of an antagonism that emanates from the individuals' social conditions of existence—but the productive forces developing within bourgeois society create also the material conditions for a solution of this antagonism. The prehistory of human society accordingly closes with this social formation."

DOKUMENT 2

Frederick Antal, "Über Museen in der Sowjetunion" [*On Museums in the Soviet Union*, translation of a typewritten manuscript in German], *Kritische Berichte* 4 (1976), no. 2/3: 5–11 [translated, 5–9].

Editorial note: Even when "On Museums in the Soviet Union" is a central text on museum history of the twentieth century, the manuscript remained unpublished until 1976. Perhaps it was intended to be held as a lecture for workers in Berlin, but due to the political situation in Germany after 1932, a public lecture like this seems unlikely.

The Hungarian Antal sometimes uses German terms with a slight semantic shift. These cases are highlighted accordingly. Furthermore, the language of the text was not embellished. The impression when reading the original is of hastily written down notes with many ambiguous expressions and thoughts open to many interpretations. An attempt has been made to preserve this character.

In this text, Antal exposes a revolutionary conception of the exhibition of art. Certain elements, such as historical comments accompanying the works of art, also became part of later exhibitions organized in the West. Therefore, it is difficult for today's reader to fully comprehend the innovative power of these exhibitions. Antal's report nevertheless refers to a form of the art exhibition which was abandoned just a few years after its creation and of which only a few photographs have remained, but there are also some texts written in French that give an insight into them.

[On Museums in the Soviet Union]

"The surprising first impression in the museums of the USSR is the dominating and fundamental contrast to the museums of the old bourgeois states. The works of art are not exposed according to purely artistic conceptions of style, but the real historical conceptions of style evolve before the eyes of the observer and, in fact, on the basis of historical materialism, thus developed out of the relations of production and from the class ideologies.

In light of this, explanations are necessary. In every exhibition hall where a fundamental new section begins tables are mounted on the walls with the most important economic data and statistics of production, in addition to explanations about the relations between economy and ideology. In most cases, every hall has a brief descriptive plate to explain the artistic ideology. In general, the excessive explanatory plates[1] have now been replaced by detailed information given in the catalogue.

Not only pictures are exhibited, but also sculptures, graphic art (engravings,[2] drawings), arts and crafts (for instance, porcelain, weapons, textiles, tapestry), photographs (architecture). As a result, the style can be recognized in its unity, in all of its manifestations. In short, the main principles of the exhibition are the explanation of relations of production and class ideologies and the resulting types of art at the same time. We can form a clear idea of this exhibition system and its immense difference to those in our museums with the help of adetailed description of an exhibit which was recently completed:

French Art at the Hermitage [Saint Petersburg]

The first exhibition room hosts the two main forces of the sixteenth century: knights and peasants. A knight in a mighty suit of armor sits on his horse in the middle of the hall. High up on the wall, a tremendous castle, below it the semi-plastic figure of a bent peasant cultivating the soil. Beside him, quotations of folk songs from this time, laments of the folk. On a smaller wall, there are tables detailing the division of classes in the sixteenth century, state finances, devaluation of wages. Quotations from Marx and Engels regarding this time and its classes. Citations from speeches of the third estate. In other exhibition halls, the thesis and antithesis of aristocratic and burgher art is displayed through pictures, drawings, arts and crafts. For instance, court art of Fontainebleau is exhibited as a unit.

[There are exhibited two opposite evolutionary lines] of book illustration: the death of manuscript literature in contrast to the new books with wood-

---

1 Frederick Antal erroneously used the German word "*Etiketten*" to denote "explanatory plates."

2 Throughout the whole text, Antal uses the word "Stich" (engraving), also when he means other printing techniques (etchings, lithographs, etc.).

block prints. Quotations by Erasmus, Rabelais, from speeches and addresses of the third estate et cetera, engravings with illustrations of religion and civil wars, whose economic causes are made clear with the help of tables.

[The following is] characteristic of the principles of how works of art are exhibited, artists are [presented] as unit or separated: division into two parts of the engravings by Callot[3]: courtly and popular. Division of the engravings by Bosse[4] into aristocratic and bourgeois. A whole Le Nain[5] hall: depiction of burghers' life. Distinction of art from the whole of the seventeenth century into courtly and bourgeois. At the same time, the permanent emphasis of bourgeois revolutionary auguries, of bourgeois speeches and reports.

Suppression of the feudal nobility through Richelieu—the result of which was the establishment of courtly absolutism—is illustrated through engravings. Poussin's[6] art [serves] as a sign of the full bloom of absolutism.

Time of Louis XIV[7]: distinctions are made between portraits of the court gentry, the service gentry [and] the bourgeoisie. Differentiation is also made between courtly decorative battle paintings and more naturalistic ones. In contrast to courtly splendor—in the middle [of the hall] stands the equestrian statue of Louis XIV—the vile abominations of Louis XIV and his murderers and incendiaries are shown by Dutch engravings and Dutch bourgeois pamphlets at the same time.

Then, the economic conditions in the middle of the eighteenth century are explained [through] tables of import and export [and] the growth of slave trade. Pictorial visualization of the obstacles for the bourgeoisie: the many taxes, for instance on wine, which were levied throughout its transit.

Encyclopédistes as champions of bourgeois revolution. Depiction of them in busts, engravings. Their books. Quotations from their works and those by Marx about them.

---

[3] Jacques Callot (1592–1635), it is no coincidence that the name of this artist appears first in the account. Callot's graphic works were one point of departure of Marxist analysis in history of art. It had been suspected that some of his graphic series, such as *Misères et Malheurs de la Guerre* (1632/33), show a kind of critical reflection. However, the *Miseries and Misfortunes of War* series was very differently interpreted among Marxist art historians.

[4] Abraham Bosse (1602 or 1604–1676), this graphic artist was one of the most renowned, popular and successful engravers of his time. The themes of his work range from scenes from courtly life, caricatures and other genres of illustration.

[5] Antoine Le Nain (ca. 1602–1648), Louis Le Nain (ca. 1606–1648), Mathieu Le Nain (1610–1677), these painters show the influence of Flemish painting. In their genre pictures they depict scenes of common life of peasants. With *Les Peintres de la réalité sous Louis XIII. Les Le Nain* (1862) by Champfleury a rediscovery of their art began.

[6] Nicolas Poussin (1594–1665), one of the major painters of the Baroque era, painter of the French king.

[7] Louis XIV (1638–1715), reign 1643–1715, reigned with absolute power from 1661 to 1715.

Vivid contrast: courtly-aristocratic art of Boucher[8] on the one side, the bourgeois art of Chardin[9], Greuze[10] on the other. Beside a picture by Greuze: Diderot's criticism of the picture concerned. Noel Hallé[11]: holy family depicted as bourgeois. Fragonard[12] marked as representative of the profiteering capital, of the general land factors, who were connected to the aristocracy. Engravings which illustrate the state of peasants before the revolution and the court.

The French Revolution [is], of course, treated in great length. Quotations from Marx as mottos. The events themselves depicted in engravings. Photographs based on pictures by David.[13] Caricatures pro and contra. In different halls, classicism from the time of the revolution and classicism from the emperor's time, to show how the same style turns into another because of other conceptions regarding contents: classicism becomes eroticized under Napoleon. And then another new hall: classicism becoming reactionary and clerical under Louis XVIII[14] and Charles X[15]: regarding Ingres.[16]

Styles of different social strata of the 19th century: of the industrial capital, the financial capital, the revolutionary petty bourgeoisie, the reactionary petty bourgeoisie. Thus, romanticism (industrial capital), pseu-

---

[8] François Boucher (1703–1770), one of the main representatives of the rococo style in painting. Russian aristocrats had collected French erotic art of the eighteenth century. After the socialization of the art collections of emigrants, many drawings and paintings by Boucher were transferred to the Hermitage. The exhibition of his works had different functions: they served to emphasize the decadence of aristocracy, at the same time, a contrast to the bourgeois painters influenced by the philosophers of Enlightenment was established.

[9] Jean Siméon Chardin (1699–1779), was a genre painter depicting common scenes from an urban household. His genre scenes in small format are interpreted as an expression of the urban bourgeoisie during the age of Enlightenment. The art of Chardin stands in an evolutionary line with Dutch genre painting of the seventeenth century.

[10] Jean-Baptiste Greuze (1725–1805), genre painter. The Hermitage is in possession of several main works, which show a moralizing tendency. His paintings corresponded with the didactic intentions of the new exhibitions.

[11] Noel Hallé (1711–1781), painter who, besides paintings in the style of rococo, created some works which suggest a certain sympathy for the lower classes of society.

[12] Jean-Honoré Fragonard (1732–1806), already in the bourgeois literature of the nineteenth century, Fragonard's erotic scenes had been declared as a sign of the decline of morals of the Ancien Régime. In the Soviet museums, the explanatory plates accompanying his paintings emphasized the "decadence" of his erotic scenes.

[13] Jacques-Louis David (1748–1825), only few works by David are stored in the Hermitage, such as *Sappho and Phaon* (1809), which was created after the revolutionary phase of the artist. Displaying opposite ideological main lines with original works of art was a great problem for Soviet museums, since critical and revolutionary directions in French painting had not been part of the collections. Therefore, photographs of paintings served to expound the general line of evolution.

[14] Louis XVIII (1755–1824), reign 1814–1824.

[15] Charles X (1757–1836), reign 1824–1830.

[16] Dominique Ingres (1780–1867), main representative of academic painting in classicist style of the nineteenth century.

do-romanticism, sentimental genre painting. In a hall there are sliding panels on the walls: engravings show the same motif as it is depicted by the reactionary financial capital and—if the panel is shifted—how it is depicted by the revolutionary petty bourgeoisie. For instance, love in the higher classes, the financial bourgeoisie: in the engravings by Devéria[17], Gavarni[18]; in the revolutionary petty bourgeoisie: in Daumier.[19] Or, for instance, fêtes galantes[20] in the style of the eighteenth and sixteenth centuries in contrast to the humorous engravings of a more progressively minded social stratum.

Motives of the people in the colonies. The Arabs depicted heroically or idyllically by the romanticists, in contrast to the anti-imperialistic tendency in [the engravings by artists of] the revolutionary petty bourgeoisie. However, the engravings also show the unclear thought regarding positive political aims of the revolutionary petty bourgeoisie (Charlet[21], Berenger[22]): veneration of Napoleon, the French Revolution as blurred ideals. The etchings by Gavarni and depictions of grisettes and courtesans before and after the revolution of 1848 are very interesting: after the revolution he becomes more critical. [It is] very telling that the courtesan[s] [are] now not only [depicted as] young, beautiful and happy [women], but also as [women] who got older.

Even from these few examples one realizes just how good engravings can be at illustrating the ideology of different, no longer progressive classes, since paintings and sculptures would pose a too heavy and over-growing material.

---

[17] Achille Devéria (1800–1879), painter and graphic artist. It can be assumed that his satirical lithographs were exhibited.

[18] Paul Gavarni (1804–1866), graphic artist. He is one of the main representatives of satirical art of the nineteenth century.

[19] Honoré Daumier (1808–1879), considered as a main protagonist of satirical art, was well-known in Russia. The account by Frederick Antal suggests that political and satirical art, after having exercised a great influence on the writings of liberal and left-wing art critics at the end of the nineteenth century, played an important role in the new revolutionary museum's conceptions.

[20] courtship parties

[21] Nicolaus Toussaint Charlet (1792–1845), graphic artist. Charlet depicted scenes from the Napoleonic wars in a realistic manner, which was uncommon in the idealized depiction of battles and wars.

[22] Jean-Baptiste Antoine Emile Béranger (1814–1883) [in the German original written as "Beregner"], was a member of a group of painters who, in the 1840s and early 1850s, depicted the situation of the lower classes with a certain melodramatic effect. This preliminary stage of realism in painting is called "protorealism," since its sentimental dimension contrasts with the neutral and objective realism created by Gustave Courbet in the 1850s. In Russian museums, only few works of French Proto-Realism were stored. However, the Hermitage is in possession of two paintings by Emile Béranger: *The Curious Woman* (*La Femme curieuse*) (1848) shows a young housemaid secretly studying books in the library of her employer. The scene is not free of a certain theatrical mood which is typical for bourgeois genre painting. The second picture, *The Teaching of the Mother* (*L'Enseignement de la mère*) (1856), takes up the theme of education. The two pictures corresponded perfectly with the didactic intentions of the Marxist exhibitions, since they showed the attempt of members of the middle and lower classes to strive for education.

Furthermore, depiction of the causes and the course of the revolutions of 1830 and 1848 in quotations, tables and engravings. For instance, police reports on the growth of the revolutionary movement, statistics of elections, the growth of the revolutionary movement under Louis Philippe.[23] Shortly before 1848: the growth of cities, data on workers' way of life.

On the separation of art of the different social strata, sometimes, there is a very practical division of the rooms into two parts: by loosening a fastened rope, the room can be transformed. For instance, in the time of Napoleon III,[24] the room exhibits either the industrial capital and the connected impressionism, or, if one is willing to untie the rope, the financial capital and the reactionary petty bourgeoisie, this is the terrible pictures by Gérôme[25] with naked female slaves or marble nudes with transparent veils (in the Tretyakov Gallery, a museum of Russian art in Moscow, exhibits include fashion drawings, dinner invitations as characteristics of the times of the tsars).

Furthermore, the same social layers under Napoleon III were more reactionary than under Louis Philippe and correspondingly so too was their art. For instance, a special exhibition hall shows the growing reactionary [tendency] of the School of Barbizon,[26] which did correspond to the liberal opposition in the past. And in this way, the separation of art of the different social strata is continued until French art of recent times, until Masereel and Picasso.

Another Example of an Exhibition: Modern Russian Art since 1910 in the Russian Museum in Leningrad

At the top in great writing, Lenin's remark as motto: Anarchism is liberation of the mind of the bourgeoisie. The whole late bourgeois art is understood as anachronism. Development of futurism until dadaism is exhibited on this basis. As petty-bourgeois-radical, idealistic, individualistic, snobbish, not directed against the bourgeois-capitalist system in general. Tables with the countless deadly accidents in the mines of Siberia during the same years.

---

[23] Louis Philippe (1773–1850), reign 1830–1848.

[24] Napoleon III (1808–1873), French president from 1848 to 1852; from 1852 to 1870, reign as Napoleon III.

[25] Jean-Léon Gérôme (1824–1904), archetype of the salon painter of the Second Empire, he was famous all over Europe. His canvases, often depicting female nudes in historical scenes, were not taken seriously in progressive art criticism of his time.

[26] The École de Barbizon denotes a group of French landscape painters who had invented a new style in representing nature, controversially debated before 1848. Some of its most celebrated representatives are Théodore Rousseau (1812–1867) and François Millet (1814–1875). In the later development of the school, typical depiction techniques of impressionism became visible.

Neo-primitivism characterized as nationalism on the grounds of remarks of the concerned artists themselves.[27] Russian Rousseau-like[28] pictures exhibited, with them folk woodblock prints to stir up for pogroms.

Expressionism. Petty-bourgeois-mystical (Chagall). Spiritualistic (Kandinsky), with remarks of the artists in question in the style of: the mind determines the material.[29]

Third Example: Museum of West European Art in Moscow [Museum of Modern Western Art][30]

Enormous collection of modern French art, the largest that exists in any museum. It consists of the nationalized collections of Shchukin and Morozov (incidentally, only the collections of emigrants are nationalized, only an inventory with an export ban has been taken concerning the others). Tremendous richness [of paintings by] Cézanne, Renoir, Gauguin, Van Gogh, Matisse and Picasso.[31] Each one has one or two halls dedicated to their works. Explanations are used to indicate the social basis of the artistic ideology in question. Relationships of expressionism with religious ideologies of the late bourgeoisie: in church architecture, in Christian art, shown with the help of photographs, magazines, illustrations.

---

[27] The exhibition of the Russian avant-garde art at the Russian Museum must be critically judged today. Frederick Antal mentioned it only in passing. Through the study of other reports written at the same time and with the help of documentary photographs, one gets the impression that this exhibition displayed a kind of mocking or satire. However, it is likely that this kind of underlying negative comment was an exception regarding the installations of modern art in the urban centers of the Soviet Union.

[28] In the German original this expression reads "*Rousseauhafte Bilder*," but this does not refer to Théodore Rousseau, but to Henri Rousseau (1844–1910), called *le Douanier* who was celebrated for his pictures in a naive style. During the time, when folk art was recognized as a source of influence for modern painting, Henri Rousseau was a well-known personality all over Europe and his style became one of the models for modern painting in "naive" style, or, as it was called in Russia "neo-primitive" style.

[29] Marc Chagall (1887–1985) as well as Wassily Kandinsky (1866–1944) had been committed to propagating new teaching methods in the early Soviet Union, but both emigrated to the West already in the early 1920s. Soviet art history was very critical about those who immigrated—if they were mentioned at all.

[30] During the Soviet era, the name of this museum changed several times, today it is known as Pushkin Museum of Fine Arts.

[31] Paul Cézanne (1839–1906), Auguste Renoir (1841–1919), Paul Gauguin (1848–1903), Vincent van Gogh (1853–1890), Henri Matisse (1869–1954), Pablo Picasso (1881–1973), painters. There is no information to suggest that there had been any kind of negative or mocking comment on modern painting in Moscow museums. The general conception of this exhibition of modern art had been to explain the whole period and its sociological entirety.

Italian neo-classicism as fascism. One hall with revolutionary art: Masereel,[32] Uitz,[33] Grosz,[34] Nagel.[35]

Then, changing exhibitions of revolutionary art from different countries.[36] At the moment, for instance, a well-executed exhibition of Dutch revolutionary art. The original collections, which reached from impressionism until the outbreak of the war and Picasso, are thus correctly supplemented up to the present day.

Learning Lessons from these Exhibitions and Its Criticism[37]

The general principle of these exhibitions is surely fundamentally correct and presents a radical change to the previously common exhibitions in the bourgeois states. And because this new exhibition principle is undoubtedly the right one, it is allowed to voice explicit criticism of its practical installation. In practice, a certain frequent change of mood is visible in the exhibition of works of art, which—frankly put—is grounded in a basic attitude against art; I will discuss this again later. The possibility of two extremes which, in my opinion, should be avoided, is not entirely excluded.

One of these extremes is that too many plates lead to an intellectual exhibition purely in accordance with the ideology of contents [of works of art], to an exhibition in which the good works of art get lost and in which no regard is given to quality. The danger is that a public which is not educated

---

[32] Frans Masereel (1889–1972), Belgian graphic artist who was one of the most renowned socialist artists of the twentieth century. His xylographic series, conceived without text, were popular over the world. The common industrial workers of this time regarded the scenes depicted in these woodcuts as a reflection of their own life.

[33] Béla Uitz (1887–1972), during the time of the first socialist Hungarian Republic in 1919, Uitz became famous for his posters and his revolutionary graphic art. After the fall of this republic, he emigrated to Vienna, later to Paris and in 1926 to the Soviet Union, where he became a teacher at the famous school of design VKhuTeMas (Higher Artistic Technical Studios) in Moscow. The VKhuTeMas was an avant-gardist school of industrial design and applied arts similar to the German Bauhaus in Weimar.

[34] George Grosz (1893–1959), in the early 1920s, Grosz was close to Communist ideas, but after a visit to the Soviet Union and due to other reasons, he changed his opinion. In 1932, he emigrated to the United States.

[35] Otto Nagel (1894–1967), belonged to the founding members of the German Communist party (KPD) and had always been an *artiste engagé*. During the Second World War, he was imprisoned in a concentration camp. His works show typical traits of proletarian art of the Weimar Republic.

[36] These exhibitions of foreign artists in the Museum of West European art focused on different themes and presented an individual artist or tendencies in social art of the 1920s and 1930s.

[37] The whole following subchapter seems to be an echo of a discussion of archeologists and art historians regarding the presentation of objects and their accompanying explanations in the museums, for instance about the question of the total number and size of the explanatory plates. This debate was also described in an article by a Soviet archeologist in 1931. Grinewitsch, *Museenexposition in der USSR*, 266–275.

in the arts may find great pleasure in many bad pictures—in the case that the examples have no artistic high quality, for instance Russian art of the nineteenth century. But it is possible—and here is the correction of an excessively intellectual exhibition—to support the better works of art through a better display. Otherwise, the effect is, in an unnecessary mood, not educational.

With this overly objective, overly intellectual type of exhibition, the question arises as to how thesis and antithesis should be shown in the course of the historical evolution. In my opinion, it is right to show thesis and antithesis when they are vivid and advancing social forces positioned as opponents (for instance in the eighteenth century, those which stood behind Greuze and Chardin on the one hand and Boucher on the other). Where there are not actual social forces, for instance reactionary petty bourgeoisie of the nineteenth century, the great mass of exhibited art corrupts the taste of the visitors, through their high number alone. Good art with the capability of development must not be outbid through sociological completeness; for instance romanticism through pseudo-romanticism, Delacroix[38] through Delaroche[39] and Ary Scheffer.[40] It is enough, as I have already said, to show engravings—too many pictures and sculptures are not necessary.

The other extreme in contrast to too many plates with explanations is too few plates with explanations, the principle that the works of art should speak for themselves. The observer has to create the historical reconstruction for himself. A principle which could be right, but which shows too much respect to art in many cases. At any rate, it must not be pushed so far that the Marxist exhibition, the principle of historical materialism, suffers under this and a hidden art for art's sake exhibition comes into being. An exhibition on the basis of historical materialism can be aesthetically effective and *at the same time* underline quality, being educationally effective in an artistic sense and still on the other hand consequently Marxist, which does not mean an aesthetically artistic [exhibition], and not according a certain taste. These two tendencies can surely be unified. Also works of art can and must be included as an element of Marxist exhibition principles. Only some magnificent works of art can and should be exhibited in a manner that they stand alone for themselves (for instance, *The Return of the Prodigal Son* by Rembrandt[41]).

[38] Eugène Delacroix (1798–1863), painter of *Liberty Leading the People* (1830), a main icon of the 1830 revolution.

[39] Hippolyte Delaroche (1797–1856), was a history painter with a certain predilection for erotic, dramatic and mystic effects, which attracted the bourgeois public.

[40] Ary Scheffer (1795–1858), was an emblematic painter of the Romantic movement whose style was influenced by academic classicism. His work corresponded with the taste of the bourgeois collectors.

[41] Rembrandt van Rijn (1606–1669), his *Return of the Prodigal Son* (ca. 1666–1669) is one of the most famous works in the possession of the Hermitage.

To exhibit all arts together, to give a clear picture of the artistic ideology of an epoch, as it is now common outside [meaning "in the Soviet Union"],[42] is an unconditionally right and constant principle.

Concerning results of the discussion which is evolving [in the Soviet Union] regarding the principles of exhibitions, I would like to summarizeas follows: it is sufficient to place few, but striking plates with explanations. The exhibitions should depend on them. Of course, this is difficult to achieve, especially first time round: the formulation of few, popular and scientifically accurate plates with explanations. Strictly speaking, visitors do not read many explanations. There need only be few, but arranged in such a way that one automatically reads them. And the whole placement of works of art should be based on these explanations.

My personal opinion is that photographs and very well-done reproductions (such as the Piper-prints[43] of drawings) [and] copies of statues could be exhibited together with the originals, in order to give a clear picture of a certain artistic ideology if the existing material is not sufficient. In particular, photographs of architecture are useful, like the Russian experience shows.

There are still some questions, which are already debated, [since some exhibitions] are not consequently designed. The exhibitions should not be stiff, but rather have to be flexible, dynamic, open to new developments. The technical mood of display, of course, has to be a modern-constructivist one. The possibilities of modern advertisement and of montage have to be used. There have to be extraordinarily well-done diagrams to illustrate and visualize the economic tables. This is about the art museums. Very shortly, I will speak about some other types of museums.

History museums in Leningrad and Moscow
Here, there is no need to take into consideration art as such. Thus, there are no fluctuations, but a clear and unequivocal line in the conception for the display of the objects. The problem of exhibition finds here its just solution. The forces of production and the social relationships are exhibited as a unit, especially [focusing the] ideologies. Here, the opposition between the ruling and the exploited class is [exposed] more striking than in the museums of fine art: for instance, regarding the eighteenth century, the contrast

---

[42] In the original texts it reads "*draußen*" (outside). Its sense is obscure for today's readers at first glance. Since it appears four times in the manuscript, also in the phrase following this one, it becomes clear that Antal uses the word "outside" to refer to the Soviet Union. In 1932, for Frederick Antal who still lived in Berlin, this meant "inside" an capitalist European country which was on the way to fascism, the only socialist country of the world was "outside."

[43] The German publishing house Piper was famous for its reproductions in the field of works of art.

between a salon in rococo style and, from the same time, an izba[44] of peasants without a chimney.

Remarkable exhibitions on history: for example in Leningrad: living conditions of the workers up to the revolution. Very instructive and very adept. For example, a very small room for three families belonging to the working class in old Saint Petersburg is reconstructed with a striking likeness.

Another exhibition on history: Exhibition about the history of the Commune in the Marx-Engels-Institute in Moscow: first of all, the economic reasons are displayed, and then a precise description of the day-to-day events with the help of engravings and models.

Museums of ethnography
The new is confronted with the old. With the help of photographs it is shown how the masses of peasants became revolutionary and transformed. Same at the Museum of Oriental Civilizations. Here, the same actualization is achieved which is also the final aim in museums of fine arts, but should [here] not be obtained with too simplistic means.

Anti-church museums
Photographs demonstrate the link between church and state. Often, very good installations ["*Montage*"][45], especially in Leningrad, where the exhibition is situated in the great cathedral.

Museums of the revolution
The economic causes of the revolutionary movements [are] extraordinarily precisely categorized with the help of charts, photographs and installations. All this exhibited in such dimensions in such an enormous number of halls that it is difficult to imagine.

Palace museum[46]
The cost of living and living conditions of the upper estates and those of the servants[47] are displayed on charts. In the suites of the last czar and his wife, everything is left as it was. The incredibly bad taste that reigned here is shown; one has the impression of a real mad house." [...]

[In the following text, Antal describes the efforts to develop a modern Russian art based on the cultural traditions of the European workers'

[44] Traditional Russian peasant's hut.

[45] In the German original as "Montage." The word is misleading, since here "mounting" refers to three-dimensional installations in constructivist style which were used for the interior design of the new exhibitions.

[46] In original as "*Schlossmuseum*" (castle museum). Antal describes, probably, the former residence of the czar in Saint Petersburg.

[47] German text reads "*Schlossarbeiter*" (workers in the palace).

movement using the example of the organization *Izoram* which was a collective of artists of proletarian origin in Leningrad. Frederick Antal does not mention socialist realism, because this conception was in the state of being carried through in 1932, instead he refers to the initiatives of the 1920s which focused on the creation of a modern social art. The author finally describes the Peoples' Culture Park in Moscow, the cultural events organized there and the possibilities of leisure activities for the masses (in the German edition of 1974 this whole passage has 56 lines). The account ends with a euphoric remark:]

"[...] And with this I want close. The two greatest impressions in the field of art that one can have outside[48] are the following: on the one hand, the possibilities of propaganda with the aid of modern art[49], and on the other hand the Marxist exhibitions[50] in the museums which causes ancient art to assume life and relevance"

Commentary

Frederick Antal described the Marxist exhibitions in Soviet art museums in a purely positive manner; today, judgments about this genre of exhibition are much more reserved, if not negative, in case that these museum experiments are mentioned at all.

Sometimes, attempts were made to establish a relation to the German Degenerate Art Exhibitions of 1937 and with this, strengthen the idea of analogies between all totalitarian states.[51] But can this really be justified?

During the period between 1917 and 1990, Russia was an isolated country. It was only possible to visit it as a guided group. Between 1933 and 1939, French, British and American delegations were allowed to travel through Russia. The new conception of museums is particularly well

[48] This means "in the Soviet Union."

[49] The original sentence reads: "[...] *das sind die Propagandamöglichkeiten der modernen Kunst.*" This ambiguous expression has caused a misleading translation into the French: "[...] *d'un côte les possibilités de propaganda l'art moderne" ("[...] on the one hand, the possibilities of propaganda of modern art."*) ("Des Musées en Union soviétique," *Histoire et critique des arts*, 2 (1978), December issue, p. 13). However, this is a typical misunderstanding regarding modern art in the early Soviet Union, since Soviet authorities of the 1920s regarded modern art really as an expression of the new state, but also as a medium of propaganda.

[50] The original text is here, again, a little confusing: "*marxistische Aufstellungen in den Museen.*" Since the German word "*Aufstellungen*" does not exist in a semantic relation to exhibitions in museums, the author means "*Ausstellungen*" (exhibitions).

[51] Adam Jolles, "Stalin's Talking Museum," *Oxford Art Journal* 28 (2005), n° 3: 429–455. Christoph Kivelitz, *Die Propagandaausstellung in europäischen Diktaturen. Konfrontation und Vergleich. Nationalsozialismus in Deutschland, Faschismus in Italien und die UdSSR der Stalinzeit* (Bochum: Winkler, 1999).

documented in literature written in French.[52] A visit to different museums was part of the program of guided tours. Reports which found a large reception in the West are by such prominent writers as André Gide (1936)[53] and John Steinbeck (1948).[54] Many accounts from this period criticize the exhibitions in Soviet museums or described them from an ironical point of view. For instance, John Steinbeck wrote a persiflage on the Lenin Museum in Moscow and criticized that there had been no single indication in the whole museum, overloaded with devotional objects about the life of Lenin, that Trotsky had ever existed.

It is not known how many art museums, apart from the three mentioned by Antal, were reconstructed according to the principles of Marxist exhibits. The process of reconstruction began from 1925 on. In all probability, only some sections of the great art museums were reconstructed according to the new principles. The interior architecture was in constructivist style, which was promoted—in applied arts—as a new expression of the culture of the working class. This explains the many remarks of Western visitors about the modernity of Soviet exhibitions.

Exhibitions in museums of archaeology and fine arts had seldom been described by Western visitors, who were interested, first of all, for the curiosity of the anti-church museums and the exhibitions of paintings in the sections of modern Russian art. Thus, the remarks of Frederick Antal on the socialist conception of the Hermitage and his description of the presentations of art from the Renaissance onwards constitute an exception. The Marxist exhibitions were not comprehensible for Western visitors, who were not acquainted with Marxist art history. In the West, the first scientific articles which contained elements of the new method were published in the 1930s. In light of this, the general impression of Western visitors must have been a confusing one, since they could not understand the explanations regarding the works of art and the whole conception remained obscure to them.

The Russian term for this kind of museum conception was 'talking museum' or 'self-explaining museum'. In all probability, the expression "Marxist exhibition" was not often used. Recent art historical literature shows the tendency to confuse the different types of museums, giving the reader the impression that this new way of evolving an exhibition was exclusively centered towards Stalinist political propaganda.[55] But is this condemnation really justified?

[52] Théodore Schmit [Fedir Šmit], "Les musées de l'Union des Républiques Socialistes Soviétiques," *Cahiers de la République des Lettres, des Sciences et des Arts* (1931): 206–221; Boris Legran, *La Reconstruction socialiste de l'Ermitage* (Leningrad ca. 1935). [Reprint of the first article and quotations from the second in: *Histoire et critique des arts* 2 (1978), December issue: 21–25.]

[53] André Gide, *Retour de l'U.R.S.S.* (Paris: Gallimard, 1936), 109–112.

[54] John Steinbeck, *A Russian Journal* (1948) (London, New York: Penguin Books, 2000), 34–35.

[55] Jolles, *Talking Museum*, 429–455.

In an essay by the archeologist Kostjatin Grinevitch of 1931, the creation of the first Marxist exhibits in museums of fine art and archaeology is described.[56] According to him, the first attempts to realize the new conceptions were in the years 1924 and 1925. He also evokes the discussion on the number of commentaries accompanying the exposed objects. In this respect, the text by Grinevitch deals with the same matters and problems as Antal in 1932.[57]

Since the construction of a permanent museum's exhibits needs a long time, one can presume that the project of reconstruction took place over the course of many years. Begun before the Stalin era, this project affected only some sections in the most important art museums. This reorganization was, in fact, carried out independently of the Stalinist Five-Years-Plans.[58]

It was in 1917 that this new idea to remodel the museum of fine arts came into being, but it needed until the mid 1920s to see its first realizations. The reshuffling did continue for a certain time under Stalin, but from 1935 or 1936 on, the Marxist art exhibits were dismantled.[59] Seeing Marxist commentaries close to paintings and sculptures was, perhaps, rejected by the majority of curators as well as the Russian visitors. It has been the most radical conception of fine arts' exhibitions that ever existed. It seems that it left few traces in Soviet literature after 1936.[60]

The 'talking museum' is a logical result of the occupation of art historians and archaeologists with Marxism in the 1920s. This direction was given preference by subordinated state institutions. Already in the early 1930s, the tendency towards a new kind of museum became visible. However, the interpretation regarding the transformation of Marxism in a totalitarian doctrine guided by Stalinism is difficult. The text by Antal, written shortly before the Stalinist period, represents one of the few accounts that testify a deep comprehension of the Marxist exhibitions.

---

[56] Grinewitsch, *Museenexposition in der USSR*, 266–275.
[57] See the chapter *Learning Lessons from these Exhibitions* in Antal's report.
[58] See contrary opinion in: Jolles, *Talking Museum*, 431.
[59] Pierre Gaudibert, "Muséologie marxiste ou sociologisme vulgaire?," *Histoire et critique des arts* 2 (1978), December issue: 14–18.
[60] Ibid.

INDEX OF PLATES

BIBLIOGRAPHY

The collected writings by Marx and Engels entitled *Marx Engels Werke* (MEW 1956–1990) were compared with the translations contained in *Marx Engels Collected Works* (MECW 1975–2004), which is the best source in English. An expansive collection on statements by Marx and Engels on art and literature has been printed in two volumes in German under the title *Karl Marx, Friedrich Engels: Über Kunst und Literatur* (Berlin: Dietz, 1967/68).

Academy of Arts of the USSR, Institute of Theory and History of Fine Arts, and B. V. Veimarn et al. (eds.). [General History of the Arts], 6 vols. Moscow: Iskusstvo, 1956–1966.
[German translation:] Akademie der Künste der UDSSR, B. V. Veimarn et al. (eds.), *Allgemeine Geschichte der Kunst*, 8 vols. Leipzig: Seemann, 1961–1972.

Adorno, *see* Horkheimer

Antal, Frederick. "Über Museen in der Sowjetunion." [1932] *Kritische Berichte* 4 (1976), n° 2/3: 5–11.

Antal, Frederick. "Remarks on the Method of Art History." *Burlington Magazine* 91 (1949): 49–52, 73–5.

Antal, Frederick. *Florentine Painting and Its Social Background: the Bourgeois Republic before Cosimo De' Medici's Advert to Power*. London: Routledge & Kegan Paul Ltd, 1948.

Antal, Frederick. *Hogarth and His Place in European Art*. London: Routledge & Kegan Paul Ltd, 1962.

Baxandall, Lee and Stefan Morawski. *Karl Marx and Frederick Engels on Literature and Art*. London: Pluto, 1973.

Baxandall, Michael. *Painting and Experience in 15th Century Italy. A Primer in the Social History of Pictorial Style*. Oxford: Oxford University Press, 1972.

Belting, Hans et al. *Kunstgeschichte. Eine Einführung* 7th edn. Berlin: Reimer, 2008.

Benjamin, Walter. "L'œuvre d'art à l'époque de sa reproduction mécanisée." *Zeitschrift für Sozialforschung* 5 (1936), n° 1: 40–66.

Bentmann, Reinhard, and Michael Müller. *Die Villa als Herrschaftsarchitektur*. Frankfurt a. M.: Suhrkamp, 1970.

Berg, Leo. "Kunst und Kapitalismus." *Die Zukunft* 32 (1900): 152–61.

Berger, John. *The Success and Failure of Picasso*. Harmondsworth: Penguin Books, 1965.

Bianchi Bandinelli, Ranuccio. *Organicità e astrazione*. Milano: Feltrinelli, 1956.

Blanke, *see* Hawel

Bottomore, Tom et al. (ed.). *A Dictionary of Marxist Thought*. Cambridge, MA: Harvard University Press, 1983.

Bourdieu, Pierre. *Distinction: A Social Critique on the Judgment of Taste*. London: Routledge & Kegan Paul, 1984.

Bürger, Peter (ed.). *Seminar: Literatur- und Kunstsoziologie*. Frankfurt a. M.: Suhrkamp, 1978.

Carter, Warren et al. (ed.). *Renew Marxist Art History*. London: Art Books, 2013.

Cesarini, Marco, and Fabrizio Onofri "Appunti per una teoria marxista dell'arte." *Realismo. Mensili di arte figurative* 3 (1954), n° 18–23.

Cesarini, Marco, and Fabrizio Onofri. "Per un'estetica marxista." *Realismo* 3 (1954), n° 24–25/26.

Clark, Timothy James. *Image of the People. Gustave Courbet and the 1848 Revolution*. London: Thames & Hudson, 1973.

Clark, Timothy James. *The Absolute Bourgeois. Artists and Politics in France 1848–1851*. London: Thames & Hudson, 1973.

Clark, Timothy James. *Farewell to an Idea. Episodes from a History of Modernism*. 2nd edn. New Haven, CT, London: Yale University Press, 2001.

Coulin, Jules. *Die sozialistische Weltanschauung in der französischen Malerei*. Leipzig: Klinkhardt & Biermann, 1909.

Engels *see* Marx

Engels, Friedrich. "Rascher Fortschritt des Kommunismus in Deutschland." (1844), *MEW*, vol. 2, 509–20.

Engels, Friedrich. *Peasant War* (1850), *MECW*, vol. 10, 397–481.

Farner, Konrad. *Kunst als Engagement. Zehn ausgewählte Essays*. Darmstadt, Neuwied: Luchterhand, 1973.

Feist, Peter H. *Prinzipien und Methoden marxistischer Kunstwissenschaft*. Leipzig: Seemann, 1966.

Finkelstein, Sidney. *Art and Society*. New York: International Publishers, 1947.

Fossati, Paolo and Giulio Bollati. *Storia dell'arte italiana*, 14 vols. Torino: Einaudi 1979–1983.

Fraenger, Wilhelm. *Jörg Ratgeb*. Dresden: Verlag der Kunst, 1972.

Francastel, Pierre. *Études de sociologie de l'art*. Paris: Denoël Gonthier, 1970.

Francastel, Pierre. *Art & Technology in the Nineteenth and Twentieth Centuries*. New York: Zone Books, 2000.

Fraquelli, Simonetta (ed.). *Radical Light: Italy's Divisionist Painters 1891–1910*, exhib. cat., National Gallery, London, 2008.

Fusaro, Diego. *Per una teoria dell'arte in Karl Marx*. [www.filosofico.net/esteticamarx.pdf] accessed May 12, 2017.

Gaudibert, P. "Muséologie marxiste ou sociologisme vulgaire?" *Histoire et critique des arts* 2 (1978), december issue: 14–8.

Gaughan, Martin I. "Lu Märten and the Question of a Marxist Aesthetic in 1920s Germany." *Renew Marxist Art History*. Warren Carter et al (ed.). London: Art Books, 2013, 283–95.

Grinewitsch (Grinevich), Kostjatin. "Probleme der Museumsexposition in der USSR." *Illustrierte Monatsschrift. Organ der Gesellschaft für Kulturelle Verbindung* [VOKS], *Deutsche Ausgabe*, 2 (1931), n° 10–12: 145–51. [reprinted in] Kristina Kratz-Kessemeier et al. (ed.). *Kunstgeschichte. Kommentierte Quellentexte 1750–1950*. Berlin: Reimer, 2010, 266–75.

Guillermo, Alice. *Social Realism in the Philippines*. Manila: Aspholdel, 1987.

Guillermo, Alice. "The Institutions of the Modern Art World in the Philippines." *Modernity in Asian Art*. Canberra: Wild Poeny, 1993, 116–27.

Guillermo, Alice. *Protest/Revolutionary Art in the Philippines 1970–1990*. Manila: University of the Philippines Press, 2001.

Guyau, Jean-Marie. *L'art au point de vue sociologique*. Paris: F. Alcan, 1889.

Hadjinicolaou [Chatzēnkolaou], Nicos. *Histoire de l'art et lutte des classes*. Paris: F. Maspero, 1973. [English edition] *Art History and Class Struggle*. 2nd edn. London: Pluto, 1979.

Hadjinicolaou [Chatzēnkolaou], Nicos. *Die Freiheit führt das Volk von Eugène Delacroix*. Dresden: Verlag der Kunst, 1991.

Harris, Jonathan. *The New Art History*. London: Routledge, 2001.

Hausenstein, Wilhelm. *Der nackte Mensch in der Kunst aller Zeiten und Völker*. Munich: Piper, 1913.

Hausenstein, Wilhelm. "Versuch einer Soziologie der bildenden Kunst." *Archiv für Sozialwissenschaft und Sozialpolitik* 36 (1913): 758–94.

Hauser, Arnold. *The Social History of Art*, 2 vols. London: Routledge & Kegan Paul, 1951.

Hauser, Arnold. *Mannerism. the Crisis of the Renaissance and the Crisis of Modern Art*. London: Routledge & Kegan Paul, 1965.

Hauser, Arnold. *Sociology of Art*. London: Routledge & Kegan Paul, 1982.

Hawel, Marcus, and Moritz Blanke (eds.). *Kritische Theorie der Krise*. Berlin: Dietz, 2012.

Held, Jutta (ed.). *Der spanische Bürgerkrieg und die bildenden Künste*. Hamburg: Argument, 1989.

Held, Jutta, and Norbert Schneider. *Sozialgeschichte der Malerei vom Spätmittelalter bis ins 20. Jahrhundert*. Cologne: DuMont, 1993.

Held, *see* Papenbrock

Hemingway, Andrew, and William Vaughan (eds.). *Art in Bourgeois Society, 1790–1850*. Cambridge: Cambridge University Press, 1998.

Hemingway, Andrew. *Artists on the Left: American Artists and the Communist Movement 1926–1956*. New Haven, CT, London: Yale University Press, 2002.

Hemingway, Andrew (ed.). *Marxism and the History of Art*. London: Pluto, 2006.

Hemingway, Andrew. *The Mysticism of Money. Precisionist Painting and Machine Age America*. Pittsburgh: Periscope, 2013.

Hemingway, Andrew. *Marxism and Art*. [www.oxfordbibliographies.com] accessed June 28, 2017.

Herding, Klaus. *Le réalisme comme contradiction. Visions, conflits et résistance dans l'œuvre de Courbet*. Ornans: Les Éditions du Sekoya, 2013 [French translation of *Realismus als Widerspruch*. 2nd enlarg. edn Frankfurt a. M.: Suhrkamp, 1984].

Hilpert, Thilo. *Hufeisensiedlung Britz 1926–1980: Ein alternativer Siedlungsbau der 20er Jahre als Studienobjekt*. Berlin: Technische Universität, 1980.

Hinz, Berthold. *Die Malerei im deutschen Faschismus. Kunst und Konterrevolution*. Munich: Hanser, 1974.

Horkheimer, Max, and Theodor W. Adorno. *Dialektik der Aufklärung. Philosophische Fragmente*. Amsterdam: Querido, 1947.

Hütt, Wolgang. *Düsseldorfer Malerschule*. Leipzig: Seemann, 1964.

Jolles, Adam. "Stalin's Talking Museum." *Oxford Art Journal* 28 (2005), n° 3: 429–55.

Kapr, Albert. *Schriftkunst. Geschichte, Anatomie und Schönheit der lateinischen Buchstaben*. Dresden: Verlag der Kunst, 1971.

Kivelitz, Christoph. *Die Propagandaausstellung in europäischen Diktaturen. Konfrontation und Vergleich. Nationalsozialismus in Deutschland, Faschismus in Italien und die UdSSR der Stalinzeit*. Bochum: Winkler, 1999.

Klingender, Francis Donald. *Art and the Industrial Revolution*. London: N. Carrington, 1947.

Klingender, Francis Donald. *Goya in the Democratic Tradition*. London: Sidgwick & Jackson, 1948.

Kingender, Francis Donald. *Hogarth and English Caricature*. London, New York: Transatlantic, 1944.

Kunzle, David. *The Early Comic Strip. Narrative Strips and Picture Stories in the European Broadsheet from c. 1450 to 1825*. Berkeley, Los Angeles, London: University of California Press, 1973 (History of the Comic Strip, Vol. 1).

Kunzle, David. *The History of the Comic Strip. The Nineteenth Century*. Berkeley, Los Angeles, Oxford: University of California Press, 1990.

Lalo, Charles. *L'art et la vie sociale*. Paris: Doin, 1921.

Landauer, Gustav. "Die Zukunft und die Kunst." *Die neue Zeit* 10, vol. 1 (1891): 532–35.

Legran, Boris. *La Reconstruction socialiste de l'Ermitage*. Leningrad ca. 1935. [quotations in: *Histoire et critique des arts* 2 (1978), december issue: 21–25.]

Lifshitz, Mikhail (ed.). *The Philosophy of Art of Karl Marx*. London: Pluto, 1973. [First published in the *Critics Group Series*, ed. by Angel Flores, New York, 1938.]

Lunatscharski (Lunacharsky), Anatolij V. *Die Revolution und die Kunst.* Dresden: Verlag der Kunst, 1974.

Märten, Lu. *Die Künstlerin.* Munich: Langen, 1914.

Märten, Lu. *Historisch-Materialistisches über Wesen und Veränderung der Künste.* Berlin: Junge Garde, 1921.

Märten, Lu. *Wesen und Veränderung der Formen und Künste. Resultate historisch-materialistischer Untersuchungen.* Berlin: Taifun-Verlag, 1924.

Marx, Karl, and Friedrich Engels. *Marx Engels Werke* (MEW), ed. by Institut für Marxismus-Leninismus (Berlin: Dietz 1956–1990), 43 vols.

Marx, Karl, and Friedrich Engels. *Marx Engels Collected Works* (MECW) (engl. edn. prepared jointly by Progress Publ., Moscow, Lawrence & Wishart, London, and International Publ., New York) 1975–2004, 50 vols.

Marx, Karl, and Friedrich Engels. *The German Ideology* (1846/47), *MECW,* vol. 5 (1976).

Marx, Karl, and Friedrich Engels. *Manifesto of the Communist Party* (1848), *MECW*, vol. 6 (1976), 477–519.

Marx, Karl. *The Eighteenth Brumaire of Louis Bonaparte* (1852), *MECW,* vol. 11 (1979), 99–197.

Marx, Karl. *A Contribution to the Critique of Political Economy, Part One* (1859), *MECW,* vol. 29 (1987), 257–265.

Marx, Karl. *Capital. Vol. 1* (1887), *MECW*, vol. 35 (1996).

Marx, Karl, and Friedrich Engels (Jean Fréville ed.). *Sur la littérature et l'art.* Paris: Éditions sociales internationales, 1936. [3rd enlarg. edn. Paris: Éditions sociales, 1954].

Marx, Carlos, and Friedrich Engels. *Sobre la literatura y el arte.* La Habana: Instituto Cubano del Libro, 1965 [two different editions].

Marx, Karl, and Friedrich Engels. *Über Kunst und Literatur.* Berlin: Dietz, 1967/68. 2 vols.

Marx, Karl, and Friedrich Engels (Valentino Gerratana ed.). *Sull'arte e la letteratura.* Milan: Novarra, Cooperativa del Libro Popolare, 1954.

Marx, Karl, and Friedrich Engels (Carlo Salinari ed.). *Scritti sull'arte.* Rome: Laterza, 1967.

Marx, Karl, and Friedrich Engels (Giuseppe Prestipino ed.). *Arte e lavoro: scritti di estetica.* Rome: Newton Compton, 1976.

Marx, Karl, and Friedrich Engels. *Sobre literatura e arte.* Lisbon: Estampa, 1971.

Marx, Karl, and Friedrich Engels. *Cultura, arte e literatura – textos escolhidos.* São Paulo: Expressão popular, 2010.

Masaryk, Tomás Garrigue. *Die philosophischen und sociologischen Grundlagen des Marxismus.* Vienna: Konegen, 1899.

McWilliam, Neil. *Dreams of Happiness. Social art and the French Left (1830–1850).* Princeton, NJ: Princeton University Press, 1993.

MECW, see Marx, Karl. *Marx Engels Collected Works.*

Mehring, Franz. "Der Kapitalismus und die Kunst." *Die Neue Zeit* 9,2

(1890/91): 649–653, 686–690, [also contained in] Franz Mehring. *Gesammelte Schriften*. Berlin: Dietz, 1976, vol. 12, 169–180.

MEW, see Marx, Karl. *Marx Engels Werke*.

Morris, William. "The lesser arts." (1877) *The Collected Works of William Morris*, vol. 22. London: Ongmans, Green & Comp, 1914, 3–27.

Morris, William. "Useful work versus useless toil." (1884) *The Collected Works of William Morris*, vol. 23. London: Ongmans, Green & Comp, 1915, 98–120.

Morris, William. "Art and Socialism." (1884) *The Collected Works of William Morris,* vol. 15. London: Ongmans, Green & Comp, 1915, 192–214.

Morris, William. *Rot und Grün. Reden zur Revolution in Kunst und Gesellschaft*. Passau: Rothe, 1988.

Münter, Georg. *Idealstädte. Ihre Geschichte vom 15.–17. Jahrhundert*. Berlin: Henschelverlag, 1957.

Musolino, Rocco. *Marxismo ed estetica in Italia*. Rome: Editori riuniti, 1963.

Olbrich, Harald (ed.). *Geschichte der deutschen Kunst 1890–1918*. Leipzig: Seemann, 1988.

Olbrich, Harald (ed.). *Geschichte der deutschen Kunst 1918–1945*. Leipzig: Seemann, 1990.

Onofri, *see* Cesarini

Panofsky, Erwin. "Die Entwicklung der Proportionslehre als Abbild der Stilentwicklung." *Monatshefte für Baukunst und Städtebau* 14 (1921): 188–219.

Panofsky, Erwin. "The history of the theory of human proportions as a reflection of the history of styles." *Meaning in the Visual Arts*. Garden City, New York: Doubleday, 1955, 55–107. [changed version of the article of 1921.]

Papenbrock, Martin et al. (ed.). *Kunst und Sozialgeschichte*. Pfaffenweiler: Centaurus Verlags Gesellschaft, 1995.

Pollock, Griselda. *Vision and Difference: Feminity, Feminism and Histories of Art*. London, New York: Routledge, 1988.

Previtali, Giovanni. "La periodizzazione della storia dell'arte italiana." *Storia dell'arte italiana*. Paolo Fossati et al. (eds.), 1st part, vol. 1, 3–96. Torino: G. Einaudi, 1979–1983, 3–96.

Proudhon, Pierre-Joseph. *Du principe de l'art et de sa destination sociale*. Paris: Garnier, 1865.

Raphael, Max. *Proudhon, Marx, Picasso. Trois études sur la sociologie de l'art*. Paris: Éditions Excelsior, 1933.

Raphael, Max. "Zur Kunsttheorie des dialektischen Materialismus." *Philosophische Hefte* 3 (1932): 125–152. [reprint:] Max Raphel. *Marx, Picasso*. Frankfurt a. M.: Suhrkamp, 1989, 7–72.

Raphael, Max. *Arbeiter, Kunst und Künstler*. Frankfurt a. M.: Fischer, 1975.

Raphael, Max. *Werkausgabe (Kunsttheoretische Schriften)*, 8 vol. Klaus

Binder, and Hans-Jürgen Heinrich (eds.). Frankfurt a. M.: Qumran, Campus, 1983–1987.

Raphael, Max. *Werkausgabe*, 11 vol. Hans-Jürgern Heinrich (ed.). Frankfurt a. M., Suhrkamp, 1989.

Raphael, Max. *The Demands of Art*. Princeton: Princeton University Press, 1968.

Read, Herbert. *Art and Society*. London: William Heinemann Ltd, 1937.

Reich, Emil. *Die bürgerliche Kunst und die besitzlosen Volksklassen*. Leipzig: Friedrich, 1892.

Reich, Emil. *Kunst und Moral*. Vienna: Manz, 1901.

Roberts, John. "Art Has No History! Reflections on Art History and Historical Materialism." *Art Has No History! The Making and Unmaking of Modern Art*. London: Verso, 1994, 1–36.

Rudolphi, Roderich. "Kunst und Proletariat." *Die neue Zeit* 15 (1896/97), n° 10: 316–17.

Schapiro, Meyer. *Romanesque Art*. New York: George Braziller, London: Chatto & Windus 1977. (Selected Papers 1)

Schapiro, Meyer. *Modern Art: 19th and 20th Centuries*. New York: George Braziller, London: Chatto & Windus 1979. (Selected Papes 2)

Schapiro, Meyer. *Late Antique, Early Christian and Mediaeval Art*. New York: George Braziller, London: Chatto & Windus 1979. (Selcted Papers 3).

Schapiro, Meyer. *Theory and Philosophy of Art*. New York: George Braziller, London: Chatto & Windus 1994. (Selected Papers 4)

Schapiro, Meyer. *Worldview in Painting: Art and Society*. New York: George Braziller, London: Chatto & Windus 1999. (Selceted Papers 5)

Schmit, Théodore (Fedir Šmit). "Les musées de l'Union des Républiques Socialistes Soviétiques." *Cahiers de la République des Lettres, des Sciences et des Arts* (1931): 206–21.

Schneider, Norbert. "Kunst und Gesellschaft: Der sozialgeschichtliche Ansatz." *Kunstgeschichte. Eine Einführung*. Hans Belting et al. (eds.). 7th edn Berlin: Reimer, 2008, 267–95.

Schneider, Norbert, *see* Held

Silbermann, *see* Taine

Silbermann, Alphons. "Kunstsoziologie." In *Soziologie* (*Fischer Lexikon*), Frankfurt a. M.: Fischer, 1958, 156–166.

Silbermann, Alphons (ed.). *Klassiker der Kunstsoziologie*. Munich: Beck, 1979.

Simmel, Georg. "Soziologische Aesthetik." *Die Zukunft* 17 (1896): 204–216.

Šmit, *see* Schmit

Soldini, S. (ed.). *Addio Lugano bella. Anarchia tra storia e arte. Da Bakunin al Monte Verità, da Courbet ai dada*, exhib. cat. Museo d'arte Mendrisio, 2015.

Solomon, Maynard (ed.). *Marxism and Art*. Brighton: Harvester Press, 1979.

Stumberger, Rudolf. *Klassen-Bilder. Sozialdokumentarische Fotografie 1900–1945*. Constance: UVK-Verlags-Gesellschaft, 2007.

Stumberger, Rudolf. *Klassenbilder II. Sozialdokumentarische Fotografie 1945–2000*. Constance: UVK-Verlags-Gesellschaft, 2010.

Tacke, Andreas, and Franz Irsigler (eds.). *Der Künstler in der Gesellschaft. Einführung zur Künstlersozialgeschichte des Mittelalters und der Frühen Neuzeit*. Darmstadt: WBD, 2011.

Taine, Hippolyte. *Philosophie de l'art*. Paris: G. Baillière, 1865–1869.

Tomars, Adolph S. *Introduction to the Sociology of Art*. Mexiko City: [s. n.] 1940.

Vandervelde, Emile. *Essais socialistes. L'alcoolisme - la religion - l'art*. Paris, F. Alcan, 1906.

Vaughan, *see* Hemingway

Walter, Franz. *Sozialismus und moderne Kunst. Nach der neueren sozialistischen Literatur dargestellt*. Freiburg i. Br.: Herder, 1901.

Warburg, Aby. *Bildniskunst und florentinisches Bürgertum*. Leipzig: Seemann, 1902.

Werckmeister, Otto Karl. *Citadel Culture*. Chicago: Chicago University Press, 1991.

White, Harrison C., and Cynthia A. White. *Canvases and Careers. Institutional Change in the French Painting World*. New York: John Wiley & Sons, 1965.

Wick, Rainer, and Astrid Wick-Kmoch (eds.). *Kunstsoziologie. Bildende Kunst und Gesellschaft*. Cologne: DuMont, 1979.

Zschelletzschky, Herbert. *Die »Drei gottlosen Maler« von Nürnberg Sebald Beham, Barthel Beham und Georg Pencz*. Leipzig: Seemann, 1975.

SUBJECT INDEX

Words in semi-bold typeface are Marxist terms.

INDEX OF PERSONS

Hermann Baum
Schlüsselfragen großer Philosophen – Band 2
In 25 neuen Geschichten entschlüsselt
Bd. 22, 2018, 152 S., 19,90 €, br., ISBN 978-3-643-13999-3

Hermann Baum
Schlüsselfragen großer Philosophen
In 25 kleinen Geschichten neu entschlüsselt
Bd. 21, 2017, 150 S., 24,90 €, br., ISBN 978-3-643-13894-1

Edgar Morscher
Die wissenschaftliche Definition
Bd. 20, 2017, 424 S., 39,90 €, br., ISBN-AT 978-3-643-50806-5

Maria Nühlen
Kultur – also sind wir!
Eine Einführung in die Kulturphilosophie
Bd. 19, 2016, 316 S., 29,90 €, br., ISBN 978-3-643-13511-7

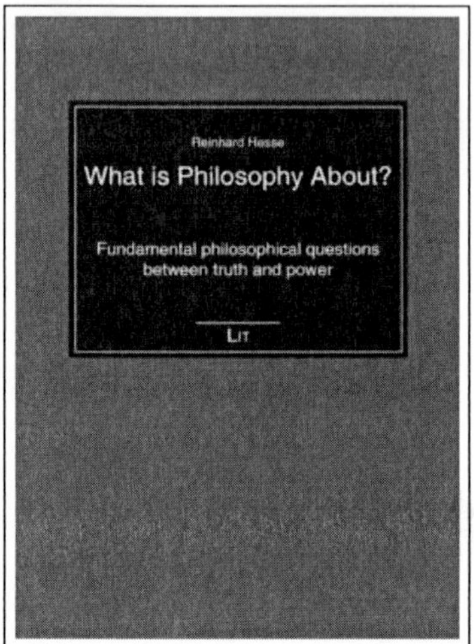

Reinhard Hesse
What is Philosophy About?
Fundamental philosophical questions between truth and power
The human being is existentially dependent on truth. Finding out the truth requires the recognition of ethical rules (of dialogue). Power is grounded on and aims for inequality. There is an inevitable tension and a tendency towards mutual subversion between power and the search for truth. It is shown why a non-argumentative search for truth (for example, in the form of religious belief) is dependent on power and why the egalitarian postulates of the ethics of dialogue lead to a political economy compatible with them.
vol. 18, 2016, 100 pp., 29,90 €, gb., ISBN-CH 978-3-643-80221-7

Gerd Garmaier
Geschichte & Philosophie. Antike
Lehrbuch zur Philosophie für das Bachelor-Studium
Bd. 17, 2012, 184 S., 19,90 €, br., ISBN 978-3-643-11781-6

LIT Verlag Berlin – Münster – Wien – Zürich – London
Auslieferung Deutschland / Österreich / Schweiz: siehe Impressumsseite